George L. Yates

Sonlight Publishing

510 Elevated Life & Leadership

Copyright © 2023 George L. Yates
SonLight Publishing

All Rights Reserved. No part of this publication may be reproduced, stored in a retrieval system or transmitted in any form or by any means—electronic, mechanical, photocopy, recording or any other—except for brief quotations in printed reviews, without the prior permission of the author.

All Scripture quotations, unless otherwise specified, are from the Holman Christian Standard Bible ® Copyright © 2003, 2002, 2000, 1999 by Holman Bible Publishers. All rights reserved.

ISBN: 978-0-9988852-7-8

For more information, please contact:
SonC.A.R.E. Ministries
soncare.net
glyates@soncare.net

510 Elevated Life & Leadership
Volume 1

Contents

1. Empowering Leadership 7
2. External or Internal Motivators,
   Which Works Best? 9
3. Are you Treating the Cause or the Symptoms? ...11
4. Is Your Message Connecting 13
5. Six Reasons Not to be an Empire Builder 15
6. A Drop of Honey Can Destroy
   an Entire Kingdom 17
7. Are You Structured for Function? 19
8. Do You Want the People Around You
   To Perform at Their Best? 21
9. Three Tiers of a Healthy Conversation 23
10. A Culture of Appreciation & Affirmation
    Builds Productivity 25
11. Three Keys in Avoiding Organizational
    Strangulation 27
12. Respect is Earned in the Trenches 29
13. Peer-to-Peer, the Most Receptive Means of
    Accountability 30
14. Rising Above Our Own Ignorance 32
15. Encouragement Builds Confidence 34
16. Effective Leaders Inspire Confidence 36
17. No One Likes to be Told 38
18. Growth Never Takes Place in the Comfort Zone...40
19. Building Resolutionists 42
20. Changing the Habit Loop 43
21. Changing the Habit Loop 2 45
22. Building Beyond You 47
23. A Recent Experience of God in the Midst 49
24. No One Likes a Micro-Manager 51
25. Being a Debate Baker 53
26. Build Talent, Strengthen Your Organization 55

27. Attract and Attach as a Magnet 57
28. Becoming a Directional Leader 59
29. Be an Increasing Leader Not a Reducing One..... 61
30. Steps to Quality Decision Making 63
31. Leadership: You Can't Do it Alone 65
32. Getting to Know him Better 67
33. Plan for Future Generations 69
34. True Leaders Create Learning Experiences 71
35. Imitation & Leadership Development 73
36. Your Mindset of Expectation 75
37. Share the Hunger 77
38. Transformational Leadership 79
39. Change the Culture, Watch the Growth 81
40. Find the Need Before Setting Your Agenda 83
41. No Problems, Only Opportunities 85
42. Be a Spark Plug Leader 88
43. Bait the Hook before You Can Lead 90
44. Leader: The Value of Learning 92
45. Vulnerability in Leadership 94
46. Moving Away From Dependent Trust 96
47. Building Trust Is Building Integrity 98
48. Connecting to Retain 100
49. Building Connection Creates Trust 102
50. Lead Like a Discipler 104
51. The Crave Factor 106
52. Simplify Your Directives 108
53. Lead With Clarity 110
54. Tell Me More 112
55. Accepting the Brutal Facts of Reality 114
56. Creating a Culture of Discipline 115
57. Whose Mirror Are You Reflecting? 117
58. People Are Not Opposed to Change 119
59. Stretching Beyond your Comfort Zone 121
60. Stalwart & Steadfast 123

Foreward

George Yates has become a dear friend of mine. In recent years he has been working with the Alabama Baptist State Board of Missions as a Church Health Strategist. Through his ministry he has been most helpful to numerous churches across our state. He is much beloved by our people.

George has had a long illustrious ministry in various other states. His ministry background is a full and a rich one. During those years of service, George has utilized his gifts of writing to share his thoughts and insights in blogs. Those blogs represent some of the finest wisdom and clearest thinking I have ever read.

George is a truly humble man who comes across in an understated way, never promoting himself. Therefore, I, and others, encouraged him to compile his blogs into book form. As your read these works you realize the possibility of one book became four. That is a blessing to all of us.

I am delighted to recommend these books by George Yates. His personal and practical observations and insights will be an encouragement to all who read them. Whether you are a minister or a layman your life will be enriched by the writings of a man who is fully devoted to Christ and His churches.

Dr. Rick Lance, Executive Director, Alabama Baptist State Board of Missions

Introduction

It is with great pleasure that I introduce to you in book form sixty (60) entries from the "George's Blog – Life leadership, and Church Health" website. While the title says church health, the principles and practices written about are valuable to any organization, or leader in any circumstance, at home, work, sports team, or other venue.

If you will take three to five minutes read one of these entries five days a week, and spend as little as five minutes contemplating how you can implement the principle or practice from your reading that day, you can elevate your leadership and increase the effectiveness of your organization. 5 days, 10 minutes.

There are currently four volumes in this set. Each volume contains sixty articles. Reading one article each day for five days a week. Each volume has three months' worth of life altering enhancements for you.

An even greater blessing is that since the articles are principle based, you can read the same volume as many times as you wish and each time you can elevate your life and leadership to a higher level. There are three more volumes with great insight for your life as well.

If you desire more information on any topic you read in these volumes, please contact George Yates at the information on the copyright page.

May God richly bless you as you read each entry in all four volumes of 510 Elevated Life and Leadership!

George L. Yates, Individual and Organizational Health Strategist, SonC.A.R.E. Ministries.

Empowering Leadership

In the church as in many organizations leadership fails to recognize the potential of the workers/volunteers. Perhaps we are afraid "they" will not do the job the way we would. Leaders (managers) assign a task and fail to empower the people to accomplish said task. Successful leaders – true fruit producing leaders understand Empowering Leadership.

Empowering Leadership is critical to productivity, higher retention and greater morale. Empowering Leadership is more about the workers than the leader. It is empowering the people assigned a task the leverage to accomplish the task. Here are two key factors for developing an Empowering Leadership model.

1. There is no other factor where such rapid progress can be made in a relatively short time frame.

The expectations for "empowering leaders" change rapidly and consistently in growing churches/organizations.

Every leader should have an apprentice. The Apostle Paul was always looking to train the next generation of leaders. Multiplication of leadership is a great growth factor.

Every leader that invests himself into other people needs mentors who invest themselves into him or her. Even the Apostle Paul had Barnabas, Silas, the other Apostles.

2. Gift oriented leadership will produce more positive results than any other.

The more extensive our responsibility the more we need people who are interested in our personal growth, and bringing out more and more of that God-given potential. It is important that every leader has a clear understanding of his/her gifts and limitations.

We need to know our gifts and limitations because it is our responsibility to lead others to works of service using their gifts and special abilities.

We are to lead them to ministries and areas of service that fit their gifting and abilities.

If you are not willing to realize the need of others in your organization/congregation you are living in a very narrow self-minded realm. You are not trusting God and His gifting of others.

Your employees/volunteers may not come at the task the exact same way you would. – They might have a better way. Do not get wrapped up in a "my way" syndrome. Guide them, but don't rule over them with an iron fist or suppressing thumb. Empower your people to take on the task with personal pride. Then allow them the freedom to accomplish the task. You will see greater productivity, personal growth, and higher morale.

External or Internal Motivators, Which works Best?

There are two ways to motivate people today. External and internal motivation. The one used most frequently in our society is the one least used by effective leaders. The one most used, external motivation. External motivation most always has a personal, tangible benefit attached. In the professional world it might be a financial bonus, a vacation trip, a meal for two at an expensive restaurant, or any number of other carrots dangling in front of employees/volunteers.

This external motivation starts at a much younger age than the work force. We tell our kids, "Finish your chores and you can watch TV a little longer. " or "Brush your teeth and you can play an extra 15 minutes." As children grow we offer them rewards for getting good grades.

External motivation may seem to work, yet it is fleeting, only for the task immediately in front of us. One person wrote, "That's scratching people where they itch, externally." The downside of scratching an itch is it never lasts, it is fleeting relief.

Effective leaders develop means of internal or intrinsic motivation. This type motivation appeals to the inner person. A trip to Hawaii sounds really nice and certainly would motivate most people for the immediate task or time period. Intrinsic motivation on the other hand fuels a desired challenge from inside the person. Internal motivation will appeal to the competitive or cooperative drives that reside inside all people. Internal motivation will also quench the thirst of the person who desires recognition and appreciation for a job well done. Internal motivation tends to support long-term noble, selfless rewards.

I realize external motivation has its place, yet it also has its consequences, short-lived. Then the next motivator has to be equal to or greater than the last. Effective leaders will also use external motivators, but not as a primary source. Effective leaders get to know their people and discover what drives each of them. For some it might be a sense of competitiveness. For others a sense of cooperation among all involved. Most people appeal to a conglomerate achievement.

An effective leader favors internal (intrinsic) motivators and balances those with only enough external motivators to spur the internal motivators. Get to know those you work with or those in your charge (care). Explore their internal motivators, they will reveal these motivators in casual conversations. Then develop motivations that appeal to their zeal for satisfaction and accomplishment. You will be glad you did, and those in your care will elevate their opinion of your leadership.

Are You Treating the Symptoms or the Cause?

The computer stopped. It froze up and would not respond to any keystroke or click of the mouse. Being new on the job and not well-versed in computer technology, the receptionist did not know what to do. Once she realized the computer would not respond, and fearful that she would lose all of the report she had been working on, she asked for help from one of the more experienced secretaries. The secretary walked over, sat down at the receptionist's desk, made a few quick keystrokes, stood up and said, "There you are," and walked away. The receptionist was relieved and went back to work. Within a couple of hours the same thing happened to the receptionist's computer. The same scenario played out. The next day came and went and the receptionist's computer locked up again. Once again, the experienced secretary came to the rescue of the new employee.

Each time the receptionist was embarrassed and did not like pulling the secretary away from her workload. She tried to watch as the secretary freed the computer. But it was to no avail. The secretary would come in, make a few quick keystrokes and be off again. The secretary was very knowledgeable in the workings of the computer. In her mind, she was doing what needed to be done. She was correcting the problem. Or was she? Was she really correcting the problem or just the symptoms?

Frustration was setting in for both ladies. In the secretary's mind the new receptionist was not learning to avoid making the error that was causing the computer to lock up. The receptionist's frustration was with the system and that the secretary wasn't taking time to teach her how to correct the problem or to avoid it. Had the secretary taken the time to explain the unlocking procedure and possibly tried to help the receptionist discover what she was doing to cause the computer to lock up, time and frustration could have been saved for both ladies.

The teacher (secretary) was very knowledgeable. Yet one thing she was overlooking was the student (receptionist) did not yet know the basics of computer operation. Many times we do the same thing in Christian education. It is easy for those of us who have been around Christianity for a lengthy period of time to forget that many of our listeners may be new Christians or non-Christians. We must continually ask ourselves, "Do they know the essentials yet?" Many of today's Christians and church attendees exhibit biblical illiteracy and a shallow faith because we assume they know, understand, and apply more than they actually do. I attribute much of this to the teaching methods we have used for many years. We can never revisit the basics too often.

In teaching or leadership in general, we need to revisit the basics of our own leadership to insure we are teaching/leading, not simply treating the symptoms. You can purchase an air freshener for your home, or you can purchase an odor eliminator. Their packaging looks very similar on store shelves. One, the air freshener sprays a heavy scent on top of the existing odors attempting to mask or hide the odors. This is treating the symptoms. It does not eliminate the original odor.

The odor eliminator (as Febreze) actually has molecules that encapsulate the hydrocarbons of odors eliminating them from the sense of smell. This is treating the cause. In your leadership and teaching are you treating the symptoms or the cause?

Is Your Message Connecting?

In the 1980's Texas, like much of the nation, was facing an ever-growing issue, litter. Littering had gotten so bad, not only states, there was a national campaign attempting to fend off this domestic menace. One national series of ads was connecting. Each ad featured an elder native American Indian with a teardrop running his cheek at the sight of litter in streams, rivers, parks, along roadways. This series had a positive effect – except in Texas.

A research group returned these findings. Most of the littering in Texas was by 18-35 year old males. They nick-named this group "Bubba". It seems none of the attempts from the state were affecting Bubba. Not even the ads with the elder Indian and the teardrop. Bubba wasn't phased to stop littering.

Officials in the state of Texas realized their messages were not connecting with "Bubba". What could be done to connect with this group? An extensive pursuit was under way to connect the needed message to this group and others throughout the state. What is it that this group respects and would react to positively?

A new ad campaign was implemented with the message that anyone littering was messing with Texas. And if you mess with Texas you are messing with anyone who cares about Texas. Texas athletes (Dallas Cowboys, country musicians as Willie Nelson were among those appearing in ads. The ad campaign was so successful that not only did the prideful Texans 18-35 (and all ages) stop littering, Bubba was willing to call anyone out whom they saw littering. Litter in Texas dropped by 72% over the next five years. The tag line that became a statewide slogan, "Don't Mess With Texas!"

If you were alive and of remembering age in the eighties, you likely remember that slogan. It was broadcast all over the nation due to the success of the campaign. It was being quoted across the country. The pride of a cleaner atmosphere was spreading beyond the Lone star state. According to Wikipedia, "While the slogan was not originally intended to become a statewide cultural phenomenon, it did." It is still in use today.

The Don't Mess with Texas campaign connected the message with the consumer. Every leader needs to continuously insure his/her message is connecting for accomplishing the desired outcomes. As in the business world, in churches, the pastor's message (not only in the pulpit) often doesn't connect with the congregation, yet the pastor/leader often does not realize the disconnect. Every ministry leader, the same.

If your church/organization is not making forward progress, fulfilling its mission (the Great Commission), there is a disconnect between your leadership and constituents. Not one of us communicates as well as we believe we do.

To insure your message as a leader is connecting with your congregants, volunteers, or consumers, find a connecting point. The way you deliver your message is usually what connects to you. That may not be the same connecting point you need. In Texas the connecting point was not cleanliness or environmental care. The connecting point was pride in their home state, and protection of fellow Texans. What will you do this week to find a better connecting point for those entrusted to your leadership?

Six Reasons Not to Be an Empire Builder

John seemed to be on the fast track for his company. He was being recognized for drawing the top talent from his business competitors. His division was beginning to look like a chess board with all back row pieces. No pawns on John's team, all captivating leaders. He had assembled a team of winners, gifted, talented, frontrunners. This was a success story in the making. Or so it seemed. Within a year the wheels began to fall off. John's team was struggling to meet the demands of productivity not to mention the chasm between reality and their goals.

How could this be? Such a team of top talent. It was like having the number one draft pick for every position on the playing field. The first thought on people's minds was, "This team is too talented. With so many top talents on one team, no wonder they could not work together." But this was not the case. The biggest downfall of John's team was John. John had become an Empire Builder.

Liz Wiseman, in her book "Multipliers" shares that Empire Builders are those leaders who attract top talent, but stifle that talent by underutilizing the talent, hoarding resources, bringing in good talented people for the leader's benefit. They bring in top talent to make themselves look good. Each one of these detriments will lessen productivity until the best talented people leave due to lack of purposeful fulfillment and utilization. As word gets out it is difficult to attract quality talent.

Instead follow these six guidelines in building a fruitful winning team.

- Recruit and hire based not only on what each person can bring to the team. Hire based on how each person can complement the team and how the team can complement the talents of each member.
- Utilize the talent of each individual on the team. If you always need to be the smartest person in the

room, – you are not – you will stifle the creative flow of the combined players of your team weakening morale.
- Intentionally invite input from all team members with a genuine aim of recognizing and utilizing "best ideas", no matter where they come from on the team.
- Provide all the resources each person needs to succeed in making the team successful. Encourage individual growth in all areas of strength and potential for every team member.
- Give feedback and congratulations at every level. With every small stride made in moving the team toward its goals, congratulate both privately to the individual and publicly in front of the whole team.
- Do not take credit: Pass the credit and shoulder the responsibility. Regardless of the amount of effort you had in a success, never take credit for yourself. Always pass the credit down the line. Likewise, even if something went wrong that you had absolutely no involvement in, shoulder the responsibility.

Don't be a self-empire builder. It will cost you in the end. Instead, follow these six guidelines and you will be a people builder. Your teams will be stronger, productive, and effective in accomplishing every task and goal assigned. I guarantee it.

A Drop of Spilled Honey Can Destroy an Entire Kingdom

There once was a queen who was eating rice cakes and honey with her chief advisor on her balcony. A drop of honey landed on the balcony railing as the queen was pointing at something in the distance. Her advisor asked if he should call a servant to clean it up, but the queen only laughed and told him that it was not her problem. "It is only a drop of honey and someone will clean it later."

As they continued eating and chatting the honey began to slowly fall to the busy street below. Once again, the advisor called attention of the queen to the honey now fallen into the street and "is now attracting flies. Shall I call for a servant." Just as before, the queen sluggishly replied, "A little drop of honey swarmed by a few flies is not my problem." She added, "Someone will deal with it later."

Soon, a lizard rushed out from underneath the palace wall and began to catch flies with its tongue. Then a cat sprang from a nearby bakery, ready for fun! The two animals batted each other back and forth like toys until suddenly, an angry butcher's dog came charging at them and began biting the cat. The advisor now reminded the queen that the flies attracted a lizard, which then attracted the cat who is now being attacked by a dog. Yet again, the queen stretched and shook her head. She told her advisor to relax, "Those silly fighting animals are not my concern."

When the baker saw a dog attacking his cat he ran out with his rolling pin and began hitting the dog. When the butcher heard his dog's cry, he ran out with his broom and started hitting the baker. The butcher and baker began fighting each other The other shopkeepers nearby took sides and joined the fight. When the soldiers came along, some of them knew the butcher while others knew the baker. They too took sides, and the battle just grew and grew in the streets.

People began throwing rocks at the windows, tipping over carts, hurdling a torch through a window, a fire raged and spread to the palace. The queen and her advisor were escorted out of the palace into the street below. Later that day when the fire had died out, surveying what remained of their land she stopped in front of where her balcony once stood and noticed a small puddle on the ground. She realized that it was honey and told herself that she should have cleaned it from the start. Now, all her kingdom was lost because of a drop of honey. From that day on, the queen never said, "It's not my problem!"

An effective leader should have the right mindset to act accordingly to whatever situation arises. When he does not, the suffering can be organization-wide like in the example of the queen in the story. Learning to listen and consider what others are suggesting is one of the greatest skills that all leaders should possess. Caring for the people working with you is essential to effectively lead them towards greatness. Seeking to resolve issues early will produce greater gain.

Are You Structured for Function?

Is your organization (or even your home) structured to function effectively and efficiently? All organizations have some type of structure. Unfortunately, many, perhaps the majority, do not have an efficient, effective operating structure. In the church for instance, nine out of ten healthy high performing New Testament churches have healthy efficient functioning structures. On the contrary, such an effective, efficient functioning structure is almost always missing in declining churches.

As mentioned in sentence two of the opening paragraph, most churches (and other organizations) have structure but lack an efficient functioning structure. Many of these issues are addressed in Reaching the Summit without ever mentioning the phrase organizational structure. We attempt to assist the church in realigning their structure to be a functioning biblically based organism with an effective, efficient functioning structure.

What does all this mean and what is the difference? Let's look at one scenario played out in many churches across North America. See if it fits your other organizations too. Most recruiting for lay (volunteer) positions in the church is done in the hallway on Sunday mornings. We corner someone in the hall and implore him/her to take a certain position for the coming fiscal year. Seldom do we offer training or even sufficient resources. We're only looking for a yes. Once someone says yes, we run off to fill the next position.

This recruiting leads to untrained or under-trained, unmotivated and sometimes unskilled people leading the ministry positions and discipleship classes in our churches. Can you see where this is going? Untrained, unmotivated people with the lack of needed skillsets cannot lead or assist their ministry and your church to effective ministry. It is easy to draw the line of comparison between this recruiting practice and declining churches. These churches indeed have a recruiting process, a structure, but not an effective or efficient one.

There is an intimate connection between structure and healthy living. In fact, you could say this connection was first demonstrated in the Genesis account of creation. Verse 2 of Genesis chapter one says "the earth was without form, empty, and full of darkness." God spoke form (structure) into place and life became a reality. Every part of the creation account in Genesis demonstrates the principle that structure gives life. Even humankind, until God breathed life into man, man was not a functioning structure.

Many of our churches find themselves going through motions of action without form and void of true biblical functioning structure. The functionality of our church (and other organizational) structure has been tested these past few weeks, and the testing is not over yet. We are quite possibly only at the beginning of the testing of effective structure functionality.

As we look ahead to coming out of this covid-19 cessation, it is critical that leaders look at the changes needed in your organizational structure and begin preparing for a better, effective, efficiently functioning structure for fulfilling God's mandate through His church. Church as usual will drive you quickly into further decline. What will you do today to begin reversing decline and setting an effective, efficient functioning structure in your organization?

Do You Want the People Around You to Perform at Their Best?

A friend of mine, Greg Hill, whom I went to high school with, was recently inducted into the Kentucky Track and Field Hall of Fame. I am very proud of Greg for this achievement. He deserves it. Greg was a multi-year state champion and record holder, a three time All-American at LSU and collegiate champion with AAU records to his credit.

I too was a sprinter, but not for my school. I was the fastest student on my church track team winning at meets. I ran well enough in gym class at school to be recruited by the school's track coaches. But I would not join the track and field team at school. My main reason – Greg Hill. Hear me, it was not anything Greg did, nor was it even about Greg. He was, and is still today, a friend whom I admire for his accomplishments. The fault lay with me. I wouldn't join the team because I knew I could never beat Greg in a race. I used Greg's athleticism to keep me from being my best in high school as an athlete.

I do regret that decision and my stinkin' thinkin' back then. Today, I want to encourage and even push others around me to be their best. You might say it's what I do for a living. I have learned and practiced over the years (long since high school) that to help others to be their best, I must pursue the same for me.

Do you want the people around you to perform at their best, to be the best they possibly can? If you want others to be their best, you must first daily practice and strive to improve to be your best. If you are a leader, you will never lead people beyond your ability. Therefore, continual striving for improvement is essential. Athletes and sports teams do not become winners relying on yesteryears practice. Winning athletes and teams push themselves everyday for growth, for improvement.

What produces winning teams in sports or business, even in families, is the willingness to produce continual practice systems and procedures that align with the vision of the entity. Don Shula, retired NFL coach of the Miami Dolphins, said, *"Everything I do is to prepare people to perform to the best of their ability."* Whether it was his coaching staff or the players on the team, Shula knew that a team will not perform on game day any better than their best day of practice.

As leaders in the business world, the church, and our own families, we need a similar resolve. Our children, employees, and volunteers will never rise above the structures of practice we build into the culture of our organization (or family). If we allow slothfulness in our organization, it becomes habit. And slothful habits keep people from reaching for the heights they can achieve. I'm living proof, those slothful habits can be broken!

Looking back, I can now say that if I had competed with you, Greg Hill, you would've helped me become a better athlete and a stronger person in my teen years. I am grateful to God that He has straightened my thinking and I now let the Greg Hill's in my life build me up.

Three Tiers of a Healthy Conversation

Bill left his supervisors office somewhat depressed. After all Bill thought he was a pretty good communicator and a friendly supervisor. Yet, the scores from his direct reports' evaluations shared that his interactions were always brief, uncaring and most often negative. His reports wanted feedback. They desired to know that Bill cared more than just keeping his job. In their opinion, Bill had never carried on a conversation with any of them.

Are you aware there are three tiers to a healthy conversation? How effective are you at guiding your conversations through all three tiers?

The first or lower tier of all conversations is sort of the foundation, what the conversation is built on. This first tier is based on facts, feelings, and fears. Isn't this where your conversations begin? "How are you today?" Response: "I'm fine." (feelings). Or another Response: "Not good, my dog ran away last night." (fact and fear) or "How's the weather where you are today?" Response: "It's raining." (fact) The entry tier of conversation usually begins with fact, fear, or feelings, or any combination of the three.

The second tier of a conversation can be thought of as the exploratory or speculative tier. On this tier the conversation turns to exploring the facts, feelings or fears in the lower tier. In the church world this tier might be peppered with questions as; "In your opinion, what have been the causes of the slow decline over the past fifteen years?" or "What types of outreach have you implemented recently?"

In response to a couple scenarios above, "How are you capitalizing on the rainy weather?" or "Has your dog run away before? Where did you find him that time?" In tier two you want to help the other individual explore and unpack the possibilities related to his/her facts, fears, or feelings. Asking the right types of questions will bring your conversation out of tier one and into tier two. Tier two can also endear others to you because through these "right" questions the other person will sense that he/she is considered worthy of your time. Therefore, they will sense that you care.

Moving to the third tier of a healthy conversation might be more difficult, but it does not have to be. Tier three might be considered the tenets tier. Tenets reveal a person's beliefs, principles, and ideals. You can move any conversation to tier three by again, asking the correct type of questions. Rather than exploring the facts, fears, and feelings as in tier two, in tier three you lead the other person in discovering a path of rescue or accomplishment.

Questions in tier three can be as, "How important is it that you find your dog today?" or in the church, "What are you willing to sacrifice to see your church turn around?" or "What must you do to prepare yourself to lead your church up that long arduous hill ahead?" Tier three questions should never be accusatory or worded in a negative manner (neither should tier two questions). Instead word your questions to lead the person to optimism and a positive outcome or accomplishment.

Do your conversations move through the FET – Foundation, Exploration, and Tenet tiers? What can you work on this week to be a better conversationalist?

A Culture of Appreciation & Affirmation Builds Productivity

"My Pleasure!" Certainly, if you've eaten at any Chick-fil-a restaurant, you've heard those words – multiple times during each visit. And, in my opinion, each employee is sincere as he/she speaks those words. How do they do it? Well, Chick-fil-a raises their own employees in an incubator. No, of course not. Part of it is training. But there is much more to the sincere spoken words than training alone.

Chick-fil-a has created a culture of appreciation and affirmation, from the corporate offices to each and every store. If those doing the hiring, training, leading, and managing do not exemplify the appreciation and affirmation attributes necessary, the employees will not either. The same is true in your environment be it at the office, on the factory line, running cable, in your church or other organization. If you desire an effective, productive environment, you must create and exemplify a culture that demonstrates these and other qualities.

The more a person is affirmed, the more he will feel appreciated. The more one feels appreciated, the more productive he will be. Each time you express appreciation for one of your employees, volunteers, you are affirming him/her. Appreciation and affirmation lead to productivity and happier employees (volunteers).

While working in retail management, I could tell the type managers/leaders in every store simply by observing and interacting with the employees. I did not have to ask any questions about their "boss." Employees actions, voice tone and inflection are tells of the type manager/leader to whom they report.

As I read, research, and speak with leaders of productive organizations I find one of the common denominators is an attitude of gratitude from the leaders to the employees/volunteers. It seems the more leaders affirm and show appreciation to the workers, the more productive the workers are. Not only productivity, this attitude seems to rub off. The employees/volunteers also demonstrate an attitude of gratitude and appreciation toward their leaders and clients/customers.

Creating a culture of appreciation and affirmation doesn't take a degree or years of classroom study. It simply requires practice and a genuine spirit. One leader told me, "We say thank you a lot." Appreciation does not always mean spending money on promotions, steak dinners, and doughnuts (although those are nice). This organization, like others, found that simply saying a genuine "Thank you!" carries more weight than a box of doughnuts.

I agree and attempt to do the same thing. I say thank you a lot – and I speak genuinely when I do. When you see someone doing something right – even if it is her job, say "Thank you." When you see one person helping another, say, "Thank you." When you see someone pick up a piece of trash, even a small gum wrapper, say, "Thank You!" Creating a culture of appreciation and affirmation takes more than a thank you. But it is a great place to start. Affirm those you lead each day.

What will you do this week to improve and demonstrate your attitude of gratitude? Don't stop after one week. Creating a different culture in your organization begins with you and requires an ongoing lifestyle from you.

Three Keys in Avoiding Organizational Strangulation

The small group sat discussing options for the future of their church. Seven men and women representing the 35-37 remaining members of Ho-Hum Ecumenical Church (or HEC). Though the church had run over 300 in attendance each Sunday twenty years ago, the facilities now look like an outdated, well-worn overcoat with the current congregation. Today's discussion, like many others over the past few years centers on trying to resurrect old events and programs that were used in the church's heyday. An hour and a half later the meeting is dismissed with no decisions made. The only plans for the future are to keep meeting on Sunday morning as always.

A scenario very similar to this plays out each week in churches across North America. In time many of these churches close their doors, leaving no Christian presence in the community, no legacy that a church ever existed – except for the empty buildings. Churches and other establishments get so caught up in past exploits and observances they do not realize the self-inflicted Organizational Strangulation.

Three elements are needed for any organization to remain healthy and avoid Organizational strangulation. Faith (inspiration), Fellowship (communication), Service (action).

Faith – complete trust or confidence in someone or something most often grounded in spiritual apprehension, not proof. In the business world inspiration takes the role of faith. Faith or inspiration gives individuals the desire to invest in moving forward without full evidence of what the future holds.

Fellowship – the friendly association of people with similar interests joining together in community. In the church and business world the strength of fellowship is determined by the depth of communication. The more people of like interests communicate with one another the closer the bond of friendly association.

Service – the act of helping or assisting others. To act or to take action is to engage in some behavioral deed. Service is one person engaging in some behavioral deed on another's behalf.

The New Testament church of Jesus Christ cannot exist without faith. Faith is a preeminence of existence for the church. No one alive today was alive when Christ walked the earth. Therefore, we rely (by faith) on what has been handed down to us in written and oral form.

It is our common interest of faith in Christ that draws us into fellowship with one another. The more time we spend relating with each other, the closer we draw to one another. The more time we spend together relating to God's Word and His directives for our lives, the closer we draw to God as individuals and as a community of believers.

True faith and fellowship in Christ cannot exist without acts of service for Christ, on His behalf to others around us. Many churches live today on a pseudo faith; a self-styled faith. It is a faith derived by our own measure, not the true Word of God.

This pseudo faith is then connected to friendship instead of realistic fellowship. Today's fellowship is based on our own level of need and desire – if and when it suits me.

When pseudo faith and me-friendship co-exist true biblical service is seldom present. In these churches when true service does exist, it is usually by accident when it is thrust upon us, not us seeking service.

The members of any organization must work together to strengthen the faith which in turn leads to inspiration for accomplishing God-sized results. The Greek word for fellowship is koinonia, living together with one another's best interest at heart. Acts of service comes from a heart to help others. Determine this week to change the culture of faith, fellowship, and service in your organization. Otherwise you might find yourself in one HEC of a church.

Respect is Earned in the Trenches

The story is told of a man on horseback riding up to a group of men digging a trench with one man barking orders and threatening punishment as the battle wearied soldiers were digging. The man on the horse asked, "Why aren't you helping?"

The man retorted, "I'm in charge. These men do as I tell them. Help them yourself if you feel so strongly about it." The man climbed down from his horse and worked alongside the men until the job was finished.

Afterward the stranger congratulated the men for a job well done. Then turning to the "leader" the horseman stated, "You should notify top command the next time your rank prevents you from assisting your men and I will come up with a more permanent solution." It was at that moment that the leader recognized the stranger as none other than General George Washington.

Fruitful leadership is helping others to perform at his/her best and assist in improving their skills. Threatening, criticizing, or treating others as less than you is not leadership. You can play leader, ridicule and criticize people or you can get in the trenches with them and demonstrate true leadership. Respect is earned and the very best way to earn respect as a leader is to get in the trenches and work alongside your men.

Respect is earned through positive interactions with employees/volunteers. A good rule of thumb is to treat others as though they could surpass you in workmanship and leadership ability. Don't treat your employees/volunteers as lower than you. Treat them with respect and watch them flourish on and off the job. You can be guaranteed after that night in the trenches, those men would gladly do whatever George Washington would ask. Why? Respect.

What is your next step to become a better "respect earner"?

Peer-to-Peer, the Most Receptive Means of Accountability

In our society today, generally speaking, top-down accountability is expected. Yet top-down accountability, being held accountable by your supervisors, actually breeds unhealthy organizations. When a team member is not meeting expectations, others await the team leader or company supervisor/manager (pastor) to step in and correct the issue. When the supervisor does not, morale and productivity drop throughout the team affecting the entire organization.

We all need accountability and accountability is good. It can keep us on track with our purpose. If any team or organization is going to stick to its decisions and goals accountability is a must. In some instances, people will drift away from the team's plan, not necessarily intentionally, but due to life's circumstances. Other times a person may deviate from the team orientation seeking personal gain or gratification.

When a person gets off-track, deviates from the organization/team plan, or simply slacks off from his/her responsibility, accountability must enter into the situation. However, as mentioned above, top-down accountability does not build a healthy or best situation. Most often resentment and suppression become the biggest outcome.

Instead of top-down accountability, a much more effective approach is peer to peer accountability. Every person on each team and in every organization must buy into peer-to-peer accountability. Even if every person does not buy in, it will always produce greater results when done with respect and friendliness. I like to refer to it as friendly accountability. Patrick Lencioni, in *The Advantage* says "Peer-to-peer accountability is the primary and most effective source of accountability on a leadership team."

I believe it to be true and have taught it for every team and organization for effective friendly accountability. When team members know that each one is committed to the fulfillment and productivity of the team, they will be more confident in approaching one another with friendly suggestions and offers of assistance.

Fred admitted in one of the team sessions that he had failed to make the three phone calls assigned to him at the previous meeting. Janet, a fellow team member steps in for the accountability. "We all have things get in the way sometimes, Fred. How can I help you to be sure to take the time to make those phone calls this week? Also, what can we do as a team to help you build into your schedule the time needed for this team's assignments?"

Notice no harsh treatment, no rebuking, no belittling words were used. Only words of, first recognition of the deviation, then offers of assistance for reconciliation to the task, not necessarily to the team. Janet did not take on Fred's responsibilities, neither did she excuse them. What Janet did through their peer-to-peer association was ask Fred what it would take to get back on track with the team.

This is friendly accountability. What steps will you take this week to build friendly accountability into your organization?

Rising Above our Own Ignorance

In his book, *See You at the Top*, Zig Ziglar shares this story; "Several years ago in Columbia, South Carolina, a young cookware salesman sat In my office. It was in early December and we were talking about plans for the next year. I asked him, "How much are you going to sell next year?" With a big grin on his face he said, "I'll guarantee you one thing; I'm going to sell more than I sold this year." My comment and question was, "That's wonderful. How much did you sell this year?" He smiled again and said, "Well, I don't really know."

Somewhat intriguing, yet sad at the same time. Intriguing that this man wanted to better himself – raise his goal from year to year. Yet, it is sad that he knew not his current position nor where he had been in terms of sales. Ziglar wrote, "Here was a young man who didn't know where he was, and no idea where he had been but, *with the confidence that generally goes with ignorance, he knew where he was going.*"

Upon reading this story again this morning the question came to mind, "Are God's children, God's church today living much the same? As we plan for this year, our stated plans are to reach more people, grow more disciples, have more in attendance...yet we fail to elicit "more" than what.

Before we can set a goal of more, we must first understand where we are at – our true net worth on the subject and on God's scale. Like the young man in our story, if we do not know how many pots and pans we sold last year, how can we say confidently that we plan to sell more this year? We must first understand the reality of our present situation. Many churches do not. We know we can do better, but we focus on being alright.

The general perception is, "It's okay. This is a new year. It'll be a better year." While we are called to "wait on the Lord..." we are not expected to sit back, fold our arms, and wait for God to do the work that He has called us to. Understanding the true position of where we are individually and as a church body is only the first step and generally due to our own biases not unearthed without the assistance of an outside unbiased coach.

Let us not continue to act out of our own ignorance (not knowing), rather let us seek to understand the reality of our current position. It is then alone that we will be able to move forward with a true plan to glorify God as should be our ultimate goal.

Encouragement Builds Confidence

No matter how intelligent and skilled your people are, no one will ever reach his/her potential if they lack confidence. Effective, fruitful leaders always work to build and boost the self-esteem of their team members, knowing when people believe in themselves greater potential will be reached. As individuals reach their potential so will the organization.

In my opinion, the number one best way to build and boost self-esteem in others is the act of genuine encouragement. Encourage each individual member of your team or organization privately and in front of others. It is easy to be negative towards someone not matching the expectations of an organization. For most of us it takes a disciplined heart and mind to build up in these situations.

Instead of discouraging someone by verbally beating her down for what she is not doing efficiently, why not encourage her in what she is doing well. You can find the good if you look. The issue is we often refuse to look beyond the negative. Therefore, we act out of the negative which only lowers morale, not only the one person in question, but all who observe or work with this person.

I am not saying praise a person who is not performing adequately. Find something good in that person, encourage her in that area, then help her build on the needed performance enhancements. In doing this you will demonstrate that you care not only about the bottom-line of the organization, you will also demonstrate that you care for the development and the spirit of all individuals on your team or in your organization.

If the only thing you can find positive in Julie is that she is always early, why not start a conversation, "Julie, I notice that you are not only on time every day, you are at your station ready to go fifteen minutes early. I want to commend you for that. Also, I want you to know that you can come to me with any thoughts or suggestions on what we can do to build you into the very best you can be. What is the first thing you can think of right now that I can help you with?"

Julie may not respond that first time the way you need her to. That is okay. You can lead her with properly formulated questions to unearth and understand her needs to improve certain areas of her performance.

I am not writing about praising bad performance. Most people do not realize how they can improve, they need a little coaching. Sometimes, a "little" coaching is all it takes. Beating down, using disparaging comments never builds up.

If you desire better performance, always encourage. Find ways to encourage every member of your organization (family, church, team). Encouragement always builds confidence. Confidence generates better performance leading to effective results. Remember encouragement always builds confidence.

Effective Leaders Inspire Confidence

John F. Kennedy inspired a nation and the leaders of a space program to put a man on the moon in less than ten years. *"Ask not what your country can do for you, but what you can do for your country."* NASA moved forward with confidence.

Martin Luther King Jr. inspired a civil rights movement with a steadfast character and a speech that is still remembered fifty years later. *"I have a dream..."* Several of King's quotes remain on the pages of social media and annually captured in many news articles around the country. Many men and women have been able to advance with a strong confidence due to Mr. king's inspiration and sacrifice.

Jack Welch was a leader who knew how to inspire others to dream big and accomplish big. Jack Welch led General Electric for two decades in which GE became a global powerhouse in many areas of business. General Electric is filled with stories of man and women who moved forward with strong confidence during Jack Welch's leadership. And they continue today.

The list goes on and on. As we read of history or history in the making, great and successful leaders were and are the leaders who inspire others to reach for the best inside themselves for the good of the organization or nation. Think back on leaders you have witnessed in your lifetime. What is it about the leaders in your own life that cause you to consider them great or better than good leaders?

I believe one contributing factor you will find in all successful leaders is the ability to inspire others to reach inside him/herself and to strive with confidence to do his/her best with their God-given abilities for the organization while increasing in his/her own capabilities.

Those who utilize this leadership practice will see others rise and increase in skill and competence. Rising beyond even what the individual thought possible. The bittersweet portion of this is the leader often says goodbye to these excelling employees as they move on to greater positions with other organizations. Yet, the successful leader knows this is part of the leadership cycle and is indeed successful leadership.

An effective leader never wants to hold someone back from reaching his/her potential just to keep that person in a current position. That would be stealing confidence, not instilling it. While losing good, quality people is tough, it is very rewarding to see and hear of future accomplishments. Learning of former employees reaching far beyond they ever could have at your organization will bring a delight to any leader if you've had a hand in encouraging and inspiring that person in his/her skillset and competences.

What will you do this week to inspire others in your organization (church or family) to dig deeper, to grow confident in fulfilling their greatest potential? What will you do to improve your leadership of inspiration?

No One Likes to Be Told

Have you ever noticed that no one likes to be told – anything, but everyone loves to give their opinion? Since this is true in our society, why not ask people's opinion instead of trying to tell them something. Without a little more information, that sounds a little silly or even ridiculous, doesn't it?

What if you could take a scenario and instead of telling what needs to be done, ask properly formulated questions that lead the person(s) to make the right decision for the circumstance. You can! It takes a little training, but you can learn this invaluable leadership practice. I am blessed to work with pastors, and organizations assisting them in this leadership style.

Pastor Don called me one morning stating he had a staff member who was not performing and was causing disturbances in the church. I listened intently, wanting to learn first, is it the pastor or staff member. Is this working relationship salvageable? After listening to the history of the situation, I understood the dilemma and asked a couple of questions to before moving forward. Then I changed my line of questioning.

The pastor had said he wanted to tell her...and he listed a couple of reasons why he believed, "It was time for she and the church to part ways."

My question was, "Why do you want to tell her anything?" Pastor Don went immediately into retelling me the same things he had previously, how she and her husband were distracting God's people from His work." I listened, then repeated my question with an emphasis on the word "tell". "Why do you want to <u>TELL</u> her anything?"

It was then that Pastor caught it. Pastor Don and a team from his church had worked with me for about a year on a revitalization process. Don had watched my leadership. I had coached him on using questions instead of always telling. The second time I asked the question, Don got it and immediately queried, "I need to ask her, don't I?"

I answered yes and we began about a twenty-minute discussion, formulating questions for his interview with her. We would discuss a properly formulated question which would allow her to surface the issues. After her response, a second question would help her dig for the true source of the issues. Then Don said, "Then I need to tell her..."

I stopped him mid-sentence and asked, "You need to what?" By the end of our conversation we had worked up four or five questions for him to ask her and I stated again, "If you ask the right, properly formulated questions, she will come to the right conclusion and make the decision.

Things worked out well. The staff member did come to the right conclusion for the church and her family. She realized it was not the church, it was indeed she and her husband causing the issues. She even stated, "I believe it is time for me and the church to part ways."

When you ask the correct, properly formulated questions, people will generally make the right decisions, even in difficult discussions as the one above. Imagine what your teams and individuals could accomplish when you ask the right questions. I'm convinced, we are not asking the right questions today. What can you do to learn more about properly formulating questions to spur your team forward?

Growth Never Takes Place in the Comfort Zone

At age 21 I had a sporting accident. I tore a bleeding cartilage and shredded all the ligaments behind my left knee, so bad they could not be surgically repaired. I had surgery to remove the bleeding cartilage followed by five weeks in a soft cast. Then I went through eight weeks of rigorous workouts at a physical therapy clinic.

My therapist was nice enough. She wasn't very big, but she sure knew how to bend, torque, and maneuver that leg to the point of deep pain. I won't say that she took pleasure in delivering me to my threshold of pain, but I do remember smiles on her face while putting me through those rigors. I took the rehab seriously and faithfully worked to strengthen that leg.

My range of motion with that leg on my first visit was 12 degrees. The day I left, 120 degrees. I had set a goal of the amount of weight I would work out with and reached it. The first day the workout was free of any weight.

My Physical Therapist taught me a series of exercises to strengthen my left leg that would take about 40-45 minutes each day. The first time was without weights. Then we strapped a one pound weight around my ankle. Then two, then three...On my last day I accomplished a feat that no man, even twice my size, had ever done. I completed that same workout with forty pounds of weight strapped to my ankle. Little skinny me, maybe 129 pounds, had successfully completed all of the required exercises with forty pounds of weight around my ankle.

When I walked out of that center for the final time my left leg was much stronger than the right leg, which had never been damaged.

I went through a lot of painful days, painful workouts during that time. I did it because I had a goal in mind. I was going to be as strong as before the accident. I came out stronger.

We all face trials, struggles, and hardships in life. There will be physical ones like I faced. There will be financial hardships and struggles, mental ones too, and even spiritual trials and struggles. When we go through life's struggles, trials, and hardships, if we allow, God will lead us through them, so that we come out stronger believers and stronger proponents for His Kingdom and His power.

In the Bible, chapter 1 of the book of James tells us **Consider it a great joy, my brothers, whenever you experience various trials, ³ knowing that the testing of your faith produces endurance. ⁴ But endurance must do its complete work, so that you may be mature and complete, lacking nothing.**

If I had laid around crying about my poor knee, and how it couldn't be surgically repaired; If I had not worked out daily as instructed by my therapist, my knee would have atrophied worse than the 5 weeks in the soft-cast. It would have been a useless knee, not able to carry my weight.

I had to stretch it, work it, bend it, lift weights with it and let the Physical Therapist bend it until I was in deep pain. My leg had to be stretched beyond what was comfortable. My rehabilitation of that leg was not a one-time venture. It was day by day, every day, a 40-45 minute workout each day. So it is in life, if you want to grow you've got to be stretched – sometimes until it hurts. It is a day by day process of development. Growth never takes place in your comfort zone. God stretches us to strengthen us. The more we're stretched, the more intense our workout, the stronger we become.

When a man accepts this testing in the right way, and day by day he develops this steadfast devotion moving through each day, then day by day he will live more triumphantly and move nearer to the standard of Jesus Christ Himself.

Building Resolutionists

"Oh no. here comes Barbara again. I wonder what's wrong now. She's a real pain in my side." In his book *People are Never the Problem*, Robert Watts Jr. states, "Ignoring the real problem and treating people as though they are problems often causes them to strike out against their accusers..."

I like to say there are no problems, only opportunities. But for this article I will interchange the words issue and problem. When we treat the problem bearer as the problem, we set at least two catalysts into motion. 1) The problem bearer is put on the defensive. 2) The real issue is set aside causing it to grow.

I agree with the title of Watt's book; *People Are Never the Problem*. People are never the issue. There are people who simply cannot recognize solutions to issues (problems) when one arises. And issues certainly will arise, in every area of life. Those people who keep coming to you with issues are not problem solvers. This is why they come to their supervisor or speak with others. they do not recognize opportunities, only issues.

When we see issues as problems, we only recognize the negative effects on the surrounding people and environment. But, when we recognize issues as opportunities, we accentuate the positive, which drives us to seek resolutions.

It is wise to train people instead of bringing a "problem" to leadership, to bring a possible solution. Leaders would much rather have someone bring a possible solution to an issue. Bearers of solutions get rewarded. Bearers of problems are avoided. It's human nature.

To be effective leaders we must do our best to equip our people to reach his/her greatest potential. Part of this equipping is to avoid problems and see opportunities to improve self and the organization. What will you do this week to build the eyes of opportunity?

Changing the Habit Loop

What is the habit loop? A habit consists of three parts; a cue, a routine action, and a reward. According to Charles Duhigg in *The Power of Habit*, the cue is a trigger that tells the brain to go into automatic mode following a learned routine. The routine is a physical, mental, or emotional behavior that follows the cue. The reward is a recurring positive stimulus that tells the brain this routine is good and to be remembered. The next time the cue is introduced, you will follow the same routine desiring a similar reward.

In the first decade and a half of the 20th century good dental hygiene in America was almost non-existent. It is said the greatest detriment of our military in World War I was not the enemy but tooth decay and oral infections. In fact, the federal government declared the deficient state of dental hygiene to be a national security risk.

This began to change when a persistent inventor & salesman convinced Claude Hopkins to invest his outstanding marketing skills behind a product called pepsodent, a paste for brushing teeth for better dental hygiene. Hopkins had been the mastermind behind Quaker Oats and other now famous products such as Goodyear.

Hopkins was perhaps genius at targeting the habit loop of Americans by finding a trigger or cue then introducing them to a new or different routine – using his product and delivering a positive reward. This reward would instruct the brain that this routine was something needed regularly. "Quaker Oatmeal would give 24 hours of energy – if you take a bowl every morning." People ate it, they felt better, so this became a habit every morning. Sales for Quaker Oats skyrocketed.

His ads for pepsodent asked you to run your tongue across your teeth. "Feel that film? Pepsodent will clean that film and give you whiter teeth." Other toothpaste manufacturers had tried this same ploy, to no avail.

What made the difference? Pepsodent ingredients included a citric acid and other ingredients that left a tingling sensation in the mouth.

This sensation, still to this day, represents in our minds a fresh clean mouth and good dental hygiene. The difference was Hopkins keyed a trigger, rubbing the tongue along the teeth, and a reward at the end of the suggested routine. Other toothpastes left no reward. In less than ten years Americans rose from less than 7% brushing their teeth daily to over 65%. Pepsodent became the number one selling toothpaste for nearly forty years. That's changing the habit loop.

If you want a more effective life or organization, change the habit loop. Most every action we do daily is based on habit. You do not think of your morning routine; you just do it. You do not look at a map to go to the grocery store, you get in your car and drive. Your day follows a regimen of habits. Why is it when you pass by a familiar bowl of candy that you side step and indulge in a piece or two? It is the habit loop.

Understanding how habits work helps you control certain areas of your life and can assist leaders in affecting the habit loops of their organization. (By the way, I know you brushed your tongue along your upper front teeth as you read that statement above)

Changing the Habit Loop Part 2

As we shared previously, much of our daily actions are routine habits. Our days consist of a series of habits. Some leaders have been successful due to changing the habit loops of their constituents, employees, or customers. It does not require an in-depth study to see how political parties have used the habit loop in swaying the thought process and habits of voters. (This, in my opinion is not a good use of changing the habit loop.)

On the other hand, Tony Dungy changed the processes of coaching football with his concept of building a team of habit driven players. Dungy, over time changed the habit loops of his teams players causing them to rely on habit, not thinking – which in football often leads to overthinking and missed opportunities. His coaching practices were unusual to the game of football at the time.

Knowing that habits are difficult to break, coach Dungy realized the need to introduce new routines into the habit loop of players. Over time the new routines began to take hold. His players were beginning to implement the new routines without thinking. His teams began winning – not one team, but two NFL franchise teams.

The habit loop consists of a cue, a time, place, or preceding action that triggers the brain to enter an automatic response. Passing through the kitchen you see a plate of brownies, your brain decides you want a brownie. The cue is seeing the plate of brownies.

The second part of the loop is your response or routine. You love brownies, so your routine is to pick up a brownie as you pass by. It is an automatic response. You don't take time to contemplate it. Your routine is to eat a brownie.

Then comes the third part of the habit loop; the reward. The reward is simply that. It is the satisfying emotional compensation you get from the taste of the brownie. The reward is a positive stimulus the brain receives following the routine of the habit loop.

Because the satisfying reward was sent to the brain as a positive stimulus, the next time you see a plate of brownies you will desire a repeat of the same routine – because your brain desires that positive stimulus.

Dungy's teams focused on only a few plays instead of the traditional 200-400 plays most teams used. Instead, his teams were focused on habits. The way an opposing player lined up across the line of scrimmage, gave a cue for Dungy's players. When his players reaction followed the practiced routine, each player and the team was successful.

In the organizational world (business or church) to become more effective, ascertain and observe the reward in your members/employees. Then identify the current routine which brings about that reward. Next brainstorm with key leaders different possible routines which could bring a similar reward- positive satisfying stimulus to the brains of members/employees. You might need to experiment, try two to three different routines, to find the one that brings the desired reward.

The cue may remain the same. Finding the right routine will lead to the path of higher productivity and effectiveness. Happy Habit Hunting! And enjoy the brownies.

Building Beyond You

The last church I served in Ohio (1993-99) realized an average growth rate above ten percent each year. It was not because of me, we, the staff, had instilled principles and practices that would out last me or the other staff members in the church. Indeed it did. The church continued its climb at a similar rate for several years after my and other staff departures. While serving at that church I would have people see me at conferences or other events and query, "So, you're George Yates" (or something similar).

I never really knew how to respond to that. At least not until they explained what they meant. Usually, it was someone who had attended my former church and heard my name attached to some biblically based practice we had set up while I was on staff. Or it was someone who had heard my name from another person who had attended a conference. It was never about me, but about the health and spiritual growth of the church(es) involved. That is never from man, but always from God.

While in California, Associational Missionary, Mike Stewart and I were blessed to have a similar mindset for building a healthy organization to assist New Testament churches. When strategically developing any process or ideal these two thoughts guided our thinking and discussion. 1) How will this lead to better effectiveness in churches. And 2) We know we can live with this, but how can we implement something that will outlive both of us. It was never about the Mike & George show. It was always about the current and future health of the organization and helping churches.

God moved me from that work twelve years and 16 days ago. That association is, in my estimation, one of the strongest associations in the nation. Mike Stewart is still there, having celebrated twenty years in 2018. I can guarantee you Mike's mindset is still to build something to grow beyond him and anyone working with him today.

Fruitful organizations that last, do not build an organization around a charismatic leader. On the contrary, effective leaders build healthy organizations that continue beyond him/herself. In each of the churches and organizations listed above I can still to this day name emergent leaders who rose from the ranks of membership. I began to list them, but realized I would leave some out and the list is long.

Leaders who try to manage every part of the organization as if he is the only one who can make a decision, that leader is setting himself and the organization up for failure. Building a church or any organization around a leader and his/her personality or past experience will set the course for a downhill spiral.

When a leader strives to build an organization that is above and beyond the leader, one that will outlive the leader, emerging leaders will begin to arise from all rank and file within the organization. What needs to change in your thinking to build such an organization?

A Recent Experience of God in the Midst

Sitting in my hotel room Wednesday evening, my cell phone rang just after 8:00. The caller ID showed a pastor who is taking his church through *Reaching the Summit*. In fact, I had been with his team just two nights prior. Reaching the Summit is a year-long process where I meet once a month with the pastor and a team from his church, looking at various principles and practices of reversing declining trends in the church. Included is a Vigorous Face to Face Summit with Reality. This church (as many do) realized their need to get into the community and be the hands and feet of Jesus.

On Monday evening we had discussed the church's discovery of their perceived strengths – what they are godly-gifted at doing as a body of believers. The pastor had led the church members to determine and list these in the previous month. The church had also reached out to school administrators and the local Sheriff's office asking for their opinion on the greatest needs in the community. These are two parts of a four quadrant matrix in helping the church in determining that one thing it can do better than anyone else in the community.

Knowing the pastor was to address the church on this particular evening with the results of their community assessment (sheriff's office & school report), I presumed he might be calling for clarification about something that had been brought up in the church meeting. I was wrong.

Instead, the pastor, with controlled delight in his voice said, "I wanted to tell you what happened tonight." He went on to tell me that as they were discussing the findings in their community assessment, which included helping the poor in the community and praying for individuals in the community, a lady unknown to anyone in the church and of a distinguishingly different ethnic background walked into the church meeting.

"She came in, walked towards the front of the room, and I asked her if I could help her." The pastor shared.

Her reply was, "Yes, I need you to pray for me and I need $94 for rent."

The pastor said he froze for a moment. He realized immediately, this was God. His actual words to me were, "George, this was a test from God on the very night we were discussing what we could do for the community." My reply was, "It was not a test. It was an opportunity."

On the very night they were speaking as a church family about becoming God's witness to the community by relieving some of the true needs of the community, God sent this lady into their midst to give the church an opportunity to join God in His work.

The pastor stopped his presentation and discussion, prayed for the lady. The church then took up a collection for her and collected $146.

I do not think it will be difficult for this church to find their way to serving God in the next few months.

> What a blessing! God will give us the desires of our heart when we seek Him. And His desire is for us to join Him in His work. How about your church? Are you seeking to truly join God in His work to the people around you and your church?

No One Likes a Micro-Manager?

Most always, the stories we hear of micro-managers are negative. Actually, I cannot think of one positive reference to a micro-manager. No one enjoys being managed this way. Have you ever thought about your own management practices. When was the last time you ran a checklist to insure you were not becoming a micro-manager?

Micro-managers, without knowing it, degrade the creativity and productivity of team members, employees, or volunteers. Below are eight characteristics of a micro-manager. Which of these characteristics have you adopted or are you flirting with?

Being never quite satisfied with results – Instead of trying to find fault or a "better way", ask questions, seek out how the team (or member) arrived at their conclusion. What steps were taken? What possibilities were surfaced? What obstacles were faced and how were obstacles overcome?

Feeling frustrated because you would have done the task differently. I learned early on in my leadership life that not everyone has the same thought processes as me. Not everyone will approach an assignment the same way as I would. That does not make me right or them wrong. Therefore, I must pull back and allow them to work to the effective solution their own way. As long as the results are effectively fulfilling the desires of the project, then all is well.

Focusing on perfection to the detriment of completion and productivity. Perfectionism is over-rated. It may sometimes be okay to be articulate, but perfectionism rarely wins the day. I am not perfect, neither are you, nor is anyone. Assist people in becoming and doing the best they are capable of. Perfectionism will then take a backseat to a much more fruitful outcome.

Continuously monitoring employee progress each day at every turn of the project. No one, not even you, likes someone looking over your shoulder. Give people the freedom to work through the various steps of a project. It is okay and helpful to check in occasionally inquiring if your assistance is needed.

Not communicating the big picture, ensuring employees can't do too much on their own. Communicate the big picture of what lies ahead but leave the details of driving to those who will be in the driver's seat for implementing the project. See post "Being a Debate Baker" on this site. Like a good GPS, you can be available to give direction when needed or advise of impending obstacles. A good GPs otherwise is quiet, ready to give assistance.

Constantly criticizing how everyone works. This usually comes from someone who is afraid of his/her own shortcomings being "found-out." Overly criticizing only weakens a team or member undermining morale and creativity.

Believing that no one else can do their job as good as the boss can. Someone else is there to complete the job because you could not on your own. Do not try to always be the smartest person in the room.

Not getting input from the team. Getting input from your team is not weakness. Instead, it is a wise leader who builds trust, accountability, and ownership in every team member through their input.

Conduct a self-inventory using the eight characteristics above. Determine working on which ones needed to improve your leadership and your organization's fruitfulness.

Being a Debate Baker

Eating flour right out the bag is not tasty. While I have done it before, consuming raw eggs is not recommended and not tasty. Add to these a cup of sugar, a teaspoon of baking powder, and one of vanilla extract, still is not worthy of our tastebuds. Even mixing them all together with some water or milk will not satisfy the taste palette. However, mix them all together and bake them in the oven for 30 minutes (perhaps with a couple other ingredients), and you may come out with a delicious cake.

To complete the recipe for a tasty cake you must combine all the raw ingredients then allow them to bake for a time. Only then do you have the desired outcome of something delicious to eat. The same is true with decision making. You can pull a group of people together with all the right ingredients for a successful team, but the individual ingredients does not a team make. First, they must be combined, as you would the ingredients for a cake.

However, the secret to a successful team is what comes next. Are you, as leader, a decision maker or a debate baker? Decision makers are those leaders who generally make most of the decisions for their team/organization, then call on the team to implement the leader's decision for success. Decision makers are creativity squashers and morale crushers. The team may carry out the leader's wishes, but with disdain and unmotivated.

Debate bakers on the other hand, know how to use the combined ingredients (creativity and experience) of each team member for a quality baking process. Without the correct baking process the cake will never develop. Good healthy debate on issues and topics are the heated oven in which to bake ideas into the desired product.

Debate bakers have learned how to draw out the best qualities from individual members, how to combine the thought processes of all members and to depersonalize individual ideas in order that the team can make great productive decisions. How?

- Learn to use questions formulated to take each mind to higher levels of thought processing. Don't settle for the run of the mill, "How can we..." questions. Instead ask questions of, "What would it require for..." Questions are perhaps the greatest tool God has given us as leaders, yet we most often squander them on questions that cannot take us to the needed solution. Learn to develop open-ended thought-provoking questions.
- Know the natural thought patterns of all team members. Most people have a routine of thought patterns. Learn how each member thinks then develop your questions to challenge each person's thought processes.
- Pair team members with other members who have different thought processes and have them discuss thoughts and ideas on the topic at hand. Then have each pair present to the whole team.
- List every pair's response on a large tear sheet. Lead the entire team in a discussion of the pros and cons of each item listed using properly formulated questions. The team's discussion should lead you to the one right idea for your organization's pursuit.

A good healthy debate involves back and forth of pros and cons of ideas. Encourage debate without allowing anyone to belittle or degrade any person in the room or organization. This is the heat in the oven which produces the tasty outcomes that everyone can enjoy.

Be a debate baker for your organization, your team, and your family. Debate bakers will always produce a better tasting outcome than decision makers.

Learn more about formulating thought provoking questions in chapters 6-9, Coaching; A Way of Leadership, A Way of Life.

Build Talent, Strengthen Your Organization

Keeping with our theme from the last couple posts, how do some leaders/organizations seem to keep members/employees? Why do some churches grow and others do not? Actually, there may be several reasons, but in this article let's look at what you can do to keep people active and growing.

The following four steps can assist you in developing and keeping people engaged and growing into their greatest potential.

1, *Observe,* be observant of the individuals in your organization. Listen to what they enjoy talking about, how he/she uses his/her hands, what brings excitement to his voice, what topics does she gravitate to. Observe how each individual attacks each part of his job/ministry and varying opportunities for service. Observation is one of your best resources for helping people grow. Past performance is the best indicator of future expectations.

In your time of observation you want to look for strengths, natural abilities, and passions. These will lead you to each person's areas of potential and fields in which he/she can soar.

2, *Connect* your observations of each person with areas within the organization where he/she can grow and develop skill and proficiency. When children seem to run to a particular man or woman in your church, and that man or woman seems to connect with the children, he/she might be a good person to serve in your preschool or children's ministry. Another person with compassion for a particular group of people, may be ideal for a ministry to that people group. Many times people do not see the connection between their passions and their potential. Help people make those connections in their life.

3, *Encourage,* people to grow into their connection points as identified. Your encouragement comes not only from verbal communication, but also from supplying all the resources you can, including physical resources, supplies, conferences, educational opportunities and more. Follow up encouragement and asking what she has learned since her discovery period is always a good reinforcer of encouragement.

4, *Acknowledge* each person for his growth in the areas you have discussed and that he has undertaken. Every small stride forward is a milestone in reaching his potential and each of those small steps need to be acknowledged by leadership and others throughout the church/organization.

When you want to keep people in your organization, help them keep growing, stretching for greater potential. Great athletes never reach a point where they stop developing skill. Great scientists never stop exploring and researching after reaching a milestone in their career. Effective leaders always are encouraging people to stretch a little farther to reach a little higher, and to strive for greater heights of development.

Cause the members of your organization to continually build on their talent and you will strengthen your organization.

Attract and Attach as a Magnet

Do you consider yourself and your organization a talent magnet? That term, talent magnet is tossed around some in the business world, but truly some pastors, church leaders and churches are also church magnets. While the term is tossed around, it is not always true of those who may claim it or to whom it is attributed.

Liz Wiseman in her book "Multipliers" and Mark Miller of Chick-fil-A in his book "Talent Magnet" both ascribe to a talent magnet as one who not only attracts best talented people to their organization, but also who keep those talented people for the long term.

A magnet not only attracts but also has the power to hold on or to keep objects attached after the attraction. Think of a magnet; hold it close enough to a metal object and the object will be drawn to the magnet, without moving the magnet. This is due to the strength of the magnetic field of the magnet. The object cannot resist being drawn to the magnet and it remains attached to the magnet.

It is easy to attract top talent for your organization. Money is a good attractant in our society. While money may attract, it is not a magnet. If you can offer enough money to hire a person of top talent, someone else can offer more money to attract them away. Money is not a magnet. A nice newer facility is certainly an attractant. Yet facilities, no matter how new or technology advanced, are not magnets. Facilities carry no power to hold talent or attach people.

Often in the church we consider how profile, high power preachers or new, state of the art facilities can be a magnet that will draw men and women to our church. In the church and in any religious organization the need to be a talent magnet is to be able to attract and attach people to Jesus Christ. He said, *"If I be lifted up, I will draw all men to me."*

To be a talent magnet ourselves, we must surrender all our self-reliant motives and desires. Surrendering our own, personal desires and wants to Christ and seeking to assist every person in our organization (church) to continually reach for his/her greatest potential will allow God to build us and our church into a talent magnet organization for His cause, the greatest cause in the world. A talent magnet acts selflessly, providing resources, encouragement, and avenues for every person to grow and excel beyond even the leaders of the organization (church). This is the attaching power of the magnet.

Are you willing and ready to surrender your position over to Christ and allow Him to draw you closer to Him so that He can reach others and grow them to their greatest potential? Attract and Attach as a Magnet!

Becoming a Directional Leader

Pastor Greg mused as one of his members walked away. "Wow, that is the fifth person this morning who has commented on the changes in his/her life. Eight in the last two weeks." Actually, none of those had used the word "change". But what each had to share was a change in the way he/she was living. Five members of Greg's congregation that morning shared with him of something they had done to share Jesus with others the previous week. A change was truly happening in the congregation. A good change! "After three years, what has finally made the difference?" Greg pondered.

In the past I have written about the importance of organizational leadership. Today I want to write about guiding leadership. While organizational leadership is critical, without guiding leadership your organization will become stagnant which could lead to organizational demise. Guiding leadership is directional leadership.

To be a guiding leader, you must be on the same journey with your organization. Willing to be in the trenches. Guiding leadership is directional leadership. Not only pointing people in a direction, but leading people through the transformation by making the transformation yourself. You cannot lead people to a place you are not willing to go personally.

Have you ever taken a guided tour and known the guide to stay behind and send you on your way? No. A guide is out in front, pointing out the beauty of the journey, helping you to see and enjoy the benefits and avoid the potential pitfalls.

The church of the near future will look different than the church of the past, even the recent past. In many ways, this is not a bad thing. Leaders of the local church (not only the pastor) must be willing to embrace change in their own ways of leadership and ministry.

In the coming church a pastor still preaches, teaches and cares for his people. Some of the changes come in how pastors and congregants interact with people in the community. Our observation patterns must change, watching for opportunities to serve our local community with a completely different mindset of what to watch for. Opportunities abound. We only need to be prayerful and watchful for God's great opportunities to show His love in ways we have neglected the past 40 years. People may not tell you of a need. We need deeper listening skills, listening to the Holy Spirit for the ways we can serve.

Another mindset change is from when we see or hear of an opportunity we must act right away. In the past we might have sat on an idea. Maybe mulled it around a few days until the opportunity passed. Often without sharing the opportunity with anyone. Changing your church's operational structure to meet needs according to the giftings and passions of the church members.

In this new era when an opportunity appears, we should immediately place a phone call (or text) to one of the leaders in the church who will spring into action getting others in the church reacting to the opportunity. Helping your members find their true passions and giftings, then matching those to ministry opportunities is perhaps the greatest key to exceptional fruitful Great Commission ministry.

Regardless of your position in the church are you ready and willing to be a directional leader? What is your first order of business to become a directional leader?

Be an Increasing Leader, Not a Reducing One

I recently heard of an associate pastor who moved from one church to another. His new pastor was different. The associate pastor said when his new pastor spent time with him, the associate pastor was always waiting for the negative bomb to drop. His anticipation of some rebuke or negative comments was strong, yet it never came. In his former setting, this did not happen – ever. His former pastor was a reducing leader. His new pastor is an increasing leader, desiring to build up and encourage the associate pastor.

You might say there are two kinds of leaders in this world. Those who increase and those who reduce. Neither of these terms, increasing or reducing, have to do with the leader him/herself, but how the leader impacts those whom he leads. An organization where morale is low and turnover is high will likely have reducing leaders/managers. While all reducing managers do not intentionally operate this way, it is what they have learned and is their leadership or management practice. Reducing leaders drain the morale and capacity of others.

Some reducing leaders have the need to be the smartest person in the room (organization). This is detrimental to productivity of individuals and the organization. Reducing leaders make a habit of devaluing or negating the input of others. Multiplying leaders on the other hand understand the wisdom of combining the knowledge of everyone in the organization.

An increasing (or multiplying) leader is always investing in others, helping them discover and build on their capacity. Multiplying leaders understand there is more effective organizational productivity by increasing the capacity of knowledge, skill, and work ability in each employee or member of the organization.

People want increasing leaders, they abhor decreasing leaders coming around their work station. People are invigorated by increasing leaders and welcome his/her presence.

Not only is the sum greater than all the individuals, the capacity of each individual increases as they interact and combine energies with one another. This in turn increases the capacity of productivity within the organization.

Becoming an increasing leader (a multiplier) is a choice that anyone in any position can make.

Research shows that most organizations never get more than two-thirds of the potential productivity from its employees/members. I would venture to say that in churches that number is likely only half of that or thirty-three percent. Perhaps we need a more encompassing multiplying leadership practice in our churches as well as other organizations to increase effectiveness and productivity. Productivity in the church is to fulfill our purpose, The Great Commission.

What will you undertake this week to become a multiplier?

Steps to Quality Decision Making

Sitting in my fourth meeting in a six-month period with a leadership group that I had been contracted to assist and evaluate, I began to look around the room for Bill Murray, the actor. I was looking for him because I knew I had to be in his movie, *Groundhog Day*. Every meeting I had attended was pretty much the same. Lots of discussion on the same topic. Some good, some chasing rabbits, but no decisions were being made.

While I am certain this leadership team thought they were leading their organization, in essence they had all abandoned the bridge and gathered regularly in the galley to discuss the needs of the organization. Who's steering the ship?

I have seen this phenomenon in churches, and organizations both religious and corporate. On the DISC scale, it will drive people with a D or C personality insane. I know, I am a C. There are people in the room who want and need a decision to be made. The organization needs decisions to be made; decisions to move the organization forward.

There are steps that can be implemented to move any organization or individual forward. The following is a five-step process that you can implement in your personal life and in your team or organization that will guide you in making good, solid, quality decisions in forward moving progress.

First, identify the issue to be addressed. Remember there are no problems, only opportunities. Seeing the issue as an avenue to greater opportunity will help you focus on the positive opportunity that lies ahead.

1. Gather the pertinent information. You need the information that will assist you in making the decision with the greatest potential of forward movement with the least amount of repercussions.
2. Identify all options that will lead to the highest impact with the least amount of negative implication.

3. Ask the following three questions of your greatest potential decision options. (top 1-3 options)
    a. If we make this decision what is the absolute best that can happen?
    b. If we make this decision what is the absolute worst that can happen? (to the organization)
    c. Are we willing and able to live with the answer to "b"? Scratch out all options that you cannot answer yes to.
4. Make your decision, take action, and move forward. Looking back, second guessing will only cause your organization to falter and languish in its efforts to succeed.

I've not known an organization yet that can say they have perfected the decision-making process. However, using a formula like the one above can propel your decision-making process into quantifiable action and effectiveness in the overall organization. Some have made extraordinary strides in their decision-making process.

What is your first step in improving your decision-making process? Don't put it off. Make a decision to begin today.

Leadership: You Can't Do It Alone

Leadership cannot be practiced in a vacuum. It is not effected alone. Leadership requires others, multiple people. To be an effective leader you must have people following your lead. Position doesn't make a leader. Just because you were elected or appointed to a leadership position, does not make you a leader. As a person in leadership you should ask yourself, "Are people following me because of my leadership personality, or because of position?" If they are following because of the position or title you hold, you need to seriously consider your leadership skills and ability.

Truly effective leaders understand effective leadership stems from the followship of others. The success of any leader depends upon those who will follow. When people see value in your abilities and skills, they will follow. When people follow in this manner, you will see a productive workforce (team) and high morale amongst employees/volunteers. Retention rates soar while turnover shrinks. Every leader should have three groups of "others" assisting him/her in leadership.

First, someone to whom he or she is responsible. Every leader is responsible and accountable to someone or some group. In large corporations most leaders have a "higher up" or up-line supervisor. The CEO or president has a Board of Directors. Even the founder and owner of a small business is accountable to someone. If no one else, his business clients. Without accountability he will not keep clients. I have had pastors tell me they are accountable to no-one but God. This is dangerous, and not the plan I read in God's word, The Holy Bible. Most churches, like other organizations have a leadership accountability ladder. Every person in every organization from family to a fortune 500 corporation is accountable.

God has positioned these accountability systems in place to allow us the ability to grow and learn from others. Even if you are in an organization where you hold the highest position of leadership, find other leaders to whom you can learn and be held accountable. You will see your leadership ability grow.

Second, every leader needs a group of peers for support and discipleship. If you are a leader, you should be a disciple of leadership – healthy leadership practices. Your peers hold similar positions, either in your organization or similar organizations. These peers face similar trials and successes as you. They also can spot your weaknesses and support you in growing through those weaknesses. Your peers can be a great learning and building resource. However, a word of caution; do not build a volley of peers who will only be sympathetic moaners, agreeing with your grievances. Your group of peers should be supportive encouragers, who care enough to correct you and assist you in strengthening your effective leadership.

Third, every leader must have followers. Too many leaders see these as underlings or subjects. A leader should always view the people serving under our leadership as the individuals who will make or break our leader potential. When we view and treat these as lesser than ourselves, we are setting the organization and our own leadership on the course of failure. As a leader, your greatest desire should be to elevate the people you lead to their greatest potential. You are leading people, not numbers or statistics.

Leadership is not done in a vacuum, nor can it be accomplished alone.

Getting To Know Him Better

There was a certain old recluse who lived deep in the mountains of Colorado. When he died, distant relatives came from the city to collect his valuables. Upon arriving, all they saw was an old shack with an outhouse beside it. Inside the shack, next to the rock fireplace, was an old cooking pot and his mining equipment. A cracked table with a three-legged chair stood guard by a tiny window, and a kerosene lamp served as the centerpiece for the table. In a dark corner of the little room was a dilapidated cot with a threadbare bedroll on it.

They picked up some of the old relics and started to leave. As they were driving away, an old friend of the recluse, on his mule, flagged them down. "Do you mind if I help myself to what's left in my friend's cabin?" he asked. "Go right ahead," they replied. After all, they thought, what inside that shack could be worth anything?

The old friend entered the shack and walked directly over to the table. He reached under it and lifted one of the floor boards. He then proceeded to take out all the gold his friend had discovered over the past 53 years – enough to have built a palace. The recluse died with only one friend knowing his true worth. As the friend looked out of the little window and watched the cloud of dust behind the relative's car disappear, he said, "They should have got to know him better."

I began my message with this story last Sunday. Then shared, I have a friend, a family member, who has riches beyond this world's imagination. He wants me – and many of you – to inherit those riches. All you need to do is *get to know Him better."*

My friend, my family member, is Jesus Christ. To get to know Him better I must understand Him. He went to synagogue every sabbath. He learned as a child and beyond. He watched and prayed to His Father every day to know His Father's will. In today's society, we want to say this is what we do. Yet, how much of our spiritualness is superficial, based on what someone else told us, or what our particular brand of religion prescribes.

Jesus spoke differently. When people heard Jesus speak, they recognized a difference in His speech than the religious leaders and Rabbis (teachers). Jesus was aware that popular applause was of little value. He spoke the truth, and it caused people to turn against Him – even those in His own hometown who had watched Him grow up.

Today, many Christians, even preachers and priests want to receive the applause and comforting strokes of man. This wasn't Jesus' model. He modeled teaching the Love of God coupled with the justness of God. God's greatest attribute is love. Therefore, He must also be a "just" God. As a loving parent will not allow a child to eat only candy and ice cream due to unhealthy consequences, God acts in a just manner to protect and grow His children.

How about you? Are you getting to know Jesus better – each day? What is your daily practice to grow in relationship with God? From this day forward, will you be like the prospector's family who drove away thinking there was nothing of value. Or will you be like the trusted friend who knew all about the vast riches and where to find them?

Plan for Future Generations

About halfway through Sunday service at Friendship Missionary Baptist Church, as worshipers passed around the collection plate, a chorus of screams pierced the air. Chunks of the ceiling in the 52-year-old church came crashing down on the crowd of about 200, striking about 14, who were later treated and released from nearby hospitals. A jagged piece of the ceiling, roughly 10 feet by 10 feet, dangled from exposed wires over the back pews as deacons struggled to guide panicking worshipers from the building. "My jaw just dropped," the Rev. Antonio Logan said. "I thought, 'This can't be real.'"

Parts of this post are adapted from an article posted to the Associated Press by One News Now on July 7, 2010

Caring for old church facilities is an increasingly acute problem. As membership declines and budgets shrink, the beautiful edifices of American Christianity can feel like weights dragging down churches that are forced to spend money on maintenance and repairs instead of ministry, charity and other Gospel-derived imperatives.

A church can be an anchor for a whole neighborhood, and its loss can hurt beyond the borders of a single congregation, as a coalition of residents and preservationists in Charlotte, NC discovered when they tried to save the old Garr Memorial Church from the wrecking ball.

The building had stood for nearly 70 years, with its iconic rooftop "Jesus Saves" sign, a beacon that locals used as a landmark when giving directions. On a Wednesday in July, the old building came down after its new owners, the New Bethel Church of God in Christ, couldn't justify refurbishing the building. "It's regretful, but the economics, just the roof repair cost was just excessive," said Bobby Drakeford, a real estate developer and consultant for New Bethel. New Bethel plans to develop the property, but for churches that try to stay in their old buildings, even necessary upkeep can become a burden.

It is important for churches to plan ahead for maintenance and repairs. I encourage every church to have two special accounts set up for unforeseen expenses. First, each church should have a minimum of three months of expenses in the bank. As communities and churches have been devastated in some of our southern states by tornadoes, hurricanes or even fire, it takes several months to get back to normal. Having an emergency/contingency fund is critical.

The second account that each church should have is an emergency repair and replacement account. A roof replacement, an air handling unit or similar needed repair can cost up to $25,000. I have worked with quite a few older churches that need to have brickwork pointed and other repairs to the century old buildings. Yet, no money has been set aside.

It is difficult for some pastors and other leaders to set aside money for these type repairs when that money could be used for ministry purposes. Though, what generations past have not realized, that by setting aside some funds each year while continuing to do ministry, will assure future generations will also be able to carry on the legacy of ministry with the burdensome financial responsibility of needed repairs.

Work as if Christ is coming back today. Plan as if He is not. Do not neglect what future generations will need from your generation in ministry and resources.

True Leaders Create Learning Experiences

As leaders, we must also strive to become master teachers. One of the gifts of a master teacher is that he/she can craft a lesson in such a way that the pupils gain the desired understanding, yet never realize the lesson is being taught. It becomes an experience of learning, not a session being taught.

It has been said that our subconscious mind often learns at a quicker pace than the conscious. I first came to realize this as I studied the ways children learn. During that course of learning a case study was presented. When a family moves to a new country with a different language, it is the children who learn the new language first. The adults may attend numerous hours of class instruction over the course of several weeks attempting to learn the language. Yet, most adults still struggle in acquiring the language and its nuances.

Children on the other hand learn the language subconsciously while playing with peers their own age. The children weren't trying to learn as they played. The learning simply came involuntarily as they did what children do, play. And children master the language much more quickly than adults. In every case studied, the results were always the same. The subconscious often learns quicker than the conscious.

As leaders, teachers, we must move away from being only dispensers of knowledge to become models, mentors and organizers of learning experiences. The conscious mind only receives facts it is prepared to receive. Perhaps you have heard students come out of a classroom saying, "I'm on brain overload." It is not that his/her brain is truly overloaded. It is that the amount of facts or depth of information presented was much more than the mind was ready to receive.

I am no accountant, yet I do enjoy playing with numbers, sometimes. But to sit and listen to an accountant speak on the ins and outs of bookkeeping would remind me of screeching fingernails on a chalkboard. Accounting is deeper than my simple number crunching mind can absorb.

A good leader or teacher will learn how to arrange facts and information for easier memory recall. It is true that part of learning happens through repetition. Yet, I contend that nothing flips into your long-term memory until there is a benefit attached to the learning experience. You do not pull a map out each time you go to the grocery store, right. You do not have to because early on you realize there is a benefit to you by going to the grocer. That benefit is good tasting satisfaction.

Be a leader who creates learning experiences for those you lead. If they can realize a benefit to themselves, they will learn and be a more productive employee/volunteer.

To learn more about becoming an organizer of learning experiences, pick up a copy of Teaching That Bears Fruit by George Yates.

Imitation & Leadership Development

As a child, my nephew, Cody, wanted to be like his Dad, my brother, Jim. I remember my brother telling the story of taking Cody to the mall one day. Cody was probably four or five at the time. Since Cody wanted to be like his Dad, they dressed alike that day. Both wearing similar colored casual pants and the same colored t-shirts. As they were walking through the mall Jim noticed Cody kept dropping back, walking behind his Dad. The first couple of times Jim slowed down and called Cody to catch up. Upon Cody's dropping back one more time, Jim realized what Cody was doing. Cody was falling behind on purpose.

Not only was he dropping back, he was lining himself up directly behind his father and mimicking his father's movements. Cody wanted to be like his Dad. Upon this realization, Jim began making other, out of the way, movements and gestures. He would run his left hand through his hair. Cody did the same. If Jim put one hand in his pocket, Cody did the same. If Jim looked left, Cody followed suit. Jim kept this up for several minutes, because the one other factor he had noticed is the smiles his son was bringing to all the people in the mall who had seen this attraction that morning.

They say imitation is the greatest form of flattery. Imitation is certainly one of our two God-given learning abilities. Children learn from their parents and others, how to walk, talk, adopt particular mannerisms and much more. Leadership styles are often acquired in the same fashion.

We tend to take on the leadership traits of the leaders we have served under. Often, it is that leader or leaders who showed interest in our personal professional development. Observation is often the best teacher. We tend to take on certain traits of those we follow. Observation lends to imitation as Cody demonstrated in the mall twenty some years ago. Imitation is one of our God-given ways of learning.

Unfortunately, there also those leaders who have adopted the traits of leaders that were not appealing as an employee. While the younger may not have liked or appreciated these leadership traits, she may adopt them, because it is what was modeled to her as a leader. This unhealthy leadership trait transfer can be problematic, for the leader, the employees, and the organization.

The bright side of this is that leadership qualities and traits can be changed and improved. Every leader should continuously strive to improve and graduate to a new level of leadership. I am a proponent of every leader developing new leaders. Regardless of your position in life, you are influencing someone. Therefore, you are a leader. Your goal should be to not teach someone to be like you, but to help him/her unearth his God-given skill and to develop to his or her greatest potential. Along the way, always encouraging each one to reach levels beyond your own leadership plane.

I believe one of the highest forms of compliment is when a leader's protégé reaches heights beyond his mentor leader. Strive to be a growing leader who grows leaders.

Your Mindset of Expectation

Just shy of my 23rd birthday I shifted directions in my vocational life. I accepted a position selling vacuum cleaners – in homes. Actually, I was quite good at it and was promoted to sales trainer within one month, though I had never been comfortable speaking in front of a group of people. Within about 8 months I had purchased a franchise and was running the regional office in Nashville, TN.

At one of the company annual meetings, speaking with some of the higher ups who had been with the company several years, a bit of information was shared that I had no previous knowledge. It was revealed that at the time I started with the company, office personnel would discreetly wager on when new recruits would "wash-out" or quit the company.

All bets were against me. I was not expected to make it out of the five-day initial training. When I did graduate, the bets were how many (less than five) sales calls would I make before hanging it up and walking away. As they shared this information the three were laughing, because, at the time of my hiring no one believed I would make it. Honestly, without the grace of God, I would not have made it through.

Would you agree that our mindset, in general, is that we do not expect great things from others? In particular, let us consider your family members, close associates at work, and friends. While you may certainly desire others (your children especially) to do great things, oftentimes our expectation mindset falls far short of our desires.

Be it in public schools or private, in church settings or the workplace, our expectation mindset (our private thoughts) is seldom that those around us are up to great things. And in these same settings, we believe our private thoughts do not matter.

In reality, what you think has a powerful impact on everyone you meet and interact with. Your thoughts are being continuously communicated to those in front of you. What you think is conveyed through your facial expressions, shoulder, arm, and hand movements. Even your eyes tell the story of your thoughts. Some people try to cover these up, but many of them are compulsory, and involuntary.

Perhaps I could read the signals being given off by these office personnel when I started with the company and set out to prove them wrong. Whether or not this is true, I had people within the organization who believed I could make it. And it was their mindset expectation that prevailed. I say their mindset instead of my own, because their positive actions toward me helped me establish my mindset for success.

Your expectation mindset for yourself and others is visible to those you spend time with. What are you communicating? Will your mindset lead to body language that says, "I know you can be a success!"?

What will you do today to improve your mindset expectation of others?

Share the Hunger

Contrary to the belief of many, leadership is not something to be lorded over the masses. Looking down on those who work for you will only bring bitterness and low morale. Yet, I am confounded at many leaders who hold this position. Successful leaders are not those who reach quotas and meet deadlines. Truly successful leaders are those who strive to raise up others by helping them to find and develop their abilities. It is then that people work together for the good of the organization.

Leaders expect, even demand certain objectives and targets from their workers. Leaders believe because a person is making a wage, he/she is obligated to have a hunger for accomplishing the company objectives. This is a dangerous and fallible way of thinking. Yet, too many leaders and organizations follow this thinking as if it were a holy grail. Workers want to know that leaders share the same hunger.

Unfortunately, much of what is seen by workers of their leaders is completely different. They see higher-paid, controlling managers, closer to slave owners than leaders. Controllers waiting to pounce on the slightest error or productivity let up. I trust this is not the type leader you wish to be. If my assumption is correct, here are three features you can undertake to become a truly successful leader.

1. Show vulnerability; You are not perfect. Admit your own mistakes. Demonstrating vulnerability validates your understanding of work and related skill. Revealing vulnerability is not a weakness. Rather, it is indeed a strength and a tool for strengthening others. It may be difficult at first, but learn to display true and tangible vulnerability. Watch production of your workers soar.
2. Act according to shared values. The values of the organization should be the same for every person within, from the CEO to the newest, lowest line level worker. Organizations where leadership has a

differing set of values than the employees, cause disunity and distrust between the ranks. If lower line employees are expected to work 60-hour weeks or produce x amount, then leadership at all levels should have like expectations.
3. Always find avenues to improve yourself as a leader and provide for others to improve themselves. Every leader should have a plan for self-improvement; improving your leader and people skills as well as the skills required to perform your job at your very best. Successful organizations observe, interview, and assist employees (volunteers) in seeking out and providing opportunities for self-improvement. This can come from mentors, books, seminars, training, cross-training, and more. As a leader your self-improvement should always make others' lives better in the process.

If you want to be a truly successful leader, commit to these three features. You will never stop growing, learning, and assisting others in self-improvement as well. And I can assure you, no financial remuneration can ever come close to the delight and contentment of the outcome of this style leadership!

Transformational Leadership

A few years ago, cartoons and movies came out featuring trucks and other machines that would convert themselves (transform) into massive superpowered robots. Or at least that's my recollection. I grew up a couple decades prior to these "Transformers". I grew up with cowboys and Indians. Therefore, I admit I do not know much about these transformers. The word transform means to change. To transform is to make a total change, more than superficial, it is a radical renovation from the inside out. So, how do we apply this to leadership?

Transformational leadership consists of initiating this same type of change. It is setting out to make a conversion from the inside out, a radical and complete conversion. Transformational leadership works toward bringing change not only in the organization itself. Transformational leaders lead with the objective to empower teams, individuals, and the leader himself to do more than improve. The objective is for a radical renovation from the inside out. When a transformation like this takes place in one's life, it normally spills over into other areas of life. Making a transformation like this at work, will overflow into one's home life and other areas as well – positive overflow.

Transformational leaders motivate others to do more than they originally intended and more than they thought possible. Transformational leaders help others to set more challenging expectations for themselves and their teams. When encouraged and empowered like this by a transformational leader, people typically achieve higher performance and greater effectiveness. Again, this will overflow from the workplace into other areas of life.

Transformational leaders tend to have more committed and satisfied workers/volunteers. Why? Because transformational leaders empower and encourage. When we empower others, we are encouraging them by saying we believe in you and that you can "do this", "rise to the challenge". Empowering another person is not only encouraging them, it is giving them the authority to run ahead and accomplish the task at hand. It also means we are giving the authority to make mistakes without undue punishment or belittlement.

Empowerment is tough for some leaders, but it is necessary for transformational leaders. You cannot be a transformational leader without empowering others. Teach them what is expected, show them what can be done. Empower and encourage them to reach for heights they never dreamed possible. Then watch the transformation take place. But don't rest on your laurels. Plan and empower your own transformation as well.

Change the Culture, Watch the Growth

Apathy and disinterest had set in like a disease. It seemed no one in the church cared any longer about the true mission of the organization. Seth had been pastor for four years and he had not been able to motivate the church members to do the work of the church. "Oh, they were good at church work," Seth thought." But there is a vast distinction between church work and the work of the church. There seemed to be zero interest in the true work of the church – accomplishing their organizational mission.

"If they (the members) would only get busy and do something outside these walls," Seth pondered, "then we could see some action. We would see some change. But they won't. It's like they are waiting for me to do it all. I'm only one man. I'm not supposed to do it all."

Seth found himself in a position with many other pastors. A congregation full of apathetic, disinterested churchgoers. Seth had tried all the trending motivational techniques, to no avail. Now frustration had set in for this pastor. Reality is, apathy had crept into Seth's life as well. So, Seth made a phone call. A phone call that would change the direction of the church.

Nine months after that phone call, Seth again found himself pondering the condition of his congregation. Only things were not so bleak this time. New people were again coming into the church. People's attitudes were different, brighter, even bubbly. Change was taking place, a transformation. And the change was in the hearts of the people of the church.

When asked by a friend what the church was doing differently, Seth replied, "We're changing the culture. We're not there yet, but we are making strides and God is blessing."

In North America we have allowed a culture of complacency into our churches over the past few decades. Without realizing it, we have ushered apathy and boredom into our churches. Yes, we invited them in. And now, they're like a mangy, stray animal that will not leave your front porch.

When boredom, apathy, and disinterest enter the workplace, we have a tendency to blame the workers. Seldom do we take an inside look at the culture we, as leaders, have created. To change a culture research tells us, will take between three to five years. Changing a culture will always require doing things differently. This begins with the leadership. Leadership must be willing to make the first changes. And it begins with the way we lead.

You cannot expect change if you continue in the same leading practices. What Seth found, was someone willing to spend time with him, pouring into Seth, allowing Seth to transform his own leadership abilities. Seth's personal culture had to change before he could lead a cultural change in his church. You can do the same. Find that gifted leader who is willing to pour into you. As you come to a place of willingness to be changed, God can and will use you.

Find the Need Before Setting Your Agenda

William sat in his office looking over his agenda for the upcoming staff meeting. It is a copy of the same agenda he used last week – and the week before, and the one prior. Actually, it is the same agenda each week. Reviewing his agenda one last time before leaving his office for the staff meeting, William wondered, "What would it take to liven up our staff meeting and overflow to our congregation with excitement?"

Effective leaders use observation before setting their agenda. Their observation is always for a need, a congratulatory moment, or an area for improvement. Effective leaders use observation first. They never set an agenda trusting it to meet a need. Observation for the need comes first. When we read the letters written by the Apostle Paul in the Bible's New Testament, Paul always addressed the specific needs of each congregation. His letters are not carbon copies sent to the various churches and cities where he had ministered.

Jesus, Himself, did likewise. As He walked life's roads, He addressed the need at hand. One young (wealthy) man came to Jesus and asked what he must do to enter heaven. After some conversation, Jesus stated, "Go and sell all that you have and give to the poor. Then come follow me." Scripture tells us, the man walked away sad. He valued his possessions too much to sell or give them away.

On another occasion, a man approached Jesus with a similar question, but wanted to wait until his father died and he was able to settle his father's estate, before he would follow Jesus. Jesus reply to him was, "Let the dead bury the dead."

Why did Jesus use two differing responses with these men? Why did Jesus not tell the second man to go and sell all that he had? Jesus addressed the need in the heart of each man. The first man was wealthy and perhaps greedy. The second man wanted to continue enjoying life as he knew it. The first man was not willing to sacrifice his wealth and possessions. The second man was not willing to sacrifice the pleasures of life. Jesus addressed the need in the heart of each man, as He did with everyone he met.

One important factor of leading is understanding the necessity in selecting the proper topic of need, instruction, or guidance. In business and in life leaders become stuck in a rut. The way out of a rut is observation, look around, see what else is available. If your desire is effective production from your employees/volunteers, watch for the area of needed instruction, guidance, and encouragement.

Did Jesus start with His content, then look for someone to listen to him? No, Jesus always began with the need and then taught on overcoming that need. Perhaps, need-meeting is a primary force of effective leadership.

No Problems, Only Opportunities

Don was a member of one church where I served on staff. He truly had a servant's heart. Don had retired from a local factory and spent much of his time serving God, leading Bible studies and services in nursing homes, visiting shut-ins, and the sick in the community. I cannot remember a time when Don was not available and ready to serve in whatever capacity was needed; whether it was visiting, a demolition or refurbishing project, or driving someone to the airport or doctor's appointment. Don truly was a servant of God and it humbles me still today when I think of his selfless, faithful service to our Lord.

I begin this article with my perspective of Don Hollingsworth because he taught me a lot. When God called me away from that church, I feel Don gave me one the greatest compliments I have ever received. On our last day of service Don stood before the congregation and said, "One thing I learned from George is there are no problems in life, only opportunities." Don went on to explain what that meant in general and in his personal life.

That may not seem like what you would consider a great compliment. I was not expecting this comment, still I consider it a compliment and a testimony of living daily of how iron sharpens iron. Here was a man twenty plus years my senior, whom God was using to influence and encourage me and sometimes to humble me as well. Following his statement, I began reflecting on our four years together in ministry and could recall Don entering my office, riding in the car to a visit, or even sitting at lunch. Though I may not have realized the events when they happened, I could now recall Don entering my office and saying we have a problem, or sitting at lunch, or in the car saying something similar using the word problem. My response was always the same, "Don, we don't have a problem, we have an opportunity." Then we would begin to explore the opportunity. What did God have in mind and in store for us through this opportunity?

You may ask, "What is the difference?" The difference, I believe is huge and of cataclysmic proportion. When we look at issues and situations as problems, our efforts and outlook are only focused on the negative. No matter how we try to explain away our attitudes and actions, dealing with problems always originate from the negative plane

On the other hand when you deal only in opportunities you always deal from the positive plane. Wherever there is an opportunity there is the prospect of betterment. When we deal with opportunity our thoughts are on improvement or becoming better. It is nearly (if not always) impossible to view opportunity from a negative plane. Opportunity imparts a positive point of view and positions you for a constructive approach to your situation or issue.

When we view our situation as a problem we almost always push the reasoning to someone or some event outside of our control. "It was the economy." "Our people are not doing their job." This is human nature because we cannot view ourselves as the "problem".

However, when we deal with opportunities we always probe how we can improve our organization, ourselves, and the productivity of our employees or volunteers. Dealing with opportunities in this manner becomes a winning situation for everyone.

Even in personal life those who deal in problems will always operate out of the negative plane. "I really messed that up. I don't know what I am doing." That is certainly dealing from a negative, problematic point of view. There was certainly something wrong here. I did mess up, the opportunity is, now how can I learn from this and take action steps to improve and demonstrate that I can do this and greater things than this.

Hopefully, by now you can see this is much more than semantics or a play on words. There is an enormous difference in attitude and action toward the issue, the people involved and the desired improved outcome.

In life you are given opportunities to help yourself and others. As long as you view people or situations as problems you will never rise above a negative perspective on life. And you will never be all that God created you to be. However, once you begin to view life as a series of opportunities, not only will your life improve. You will assist in the improvement of life for many. That my friends is the purpose God has for you in life.

Remember, there are no problems in life, only opportunities. Let's improve something today!

Be a Spark Plug Leader

Though Shirley had not been looking forward to the task ahead, she walked out of her boss's office with vigor and determination to get the job done. Shirley was charged up, invigorated ready to slay the dragon. Why? What made the change in her disposition. After all, Shirley had been vocally dreading this task for two weeks. The difference came because Jane, Shirley's boss, is a spark plug leader.

Jane understands human behavior and knows her employees. She has a caring personality and demonstrates it to those who work for and with her. Jane, it seems, can make any employee feel good about themselves even in undesirable circumstances. Yet, as Shirley explains, it is much more than making you feel good. Jane has a way to make you feel you can "slay the dragon" ahead of you. Five minutes with Jane and you'll charge headlong into action, and you'll complete the task you've been dreading for months. It has happened time and time again with her coworkers and employees.

Jane is a spark plug leader. A gas engine does not run without at least one spark plug. A spark plug's purpose is to generate enough electrical energy to create an electrical spark which in turn ignites the fuel to run the engine. A spark plug leader must know his people well enough to understand what motivates him/her. This is the fuel that needs to be ignited. People are different. Therefore, the fuel that ignites one man's work passion, will likely be different from the man working next to him.

The spark plug leader learns these motivators (fuels) and through passion and a caring attitude, builds the electricity needed to ignite the fuel in each employee to charge ahead into the task that awaits. Greater results are accomplished through spark plug leaders than high octane leadership. In other words, some leaders attempt to get the fires burning in their employees/volunteers work ethic, by dousing the situation with more high-octane fuel. High octane fuel ignites quickly, but also burns out quickly.

Don't be a high-octane leader. Learn to be a spark plug leader. Effective production will increase along with morale and employee retention.

Bait the Hook before You Can Lead

Bruce Wilkinson tells a story of taking his two children, David 7 Jenny fishing for the first time. David had no problem baiting his hook with a worm. Jenny on the other hand refused to. Not accepting the fact that she needed a worm on her shiny hook to catch a fish, she walked to one end of the little pier and cast her shiny hook and bobber into the pond. Her brother on the other hand baited his hook, cast and caught a fish quickly. Jenny came running to see, but still could not be convinced to use a worm on her hook.

After David's third fish, Jenny was convinced it was his "lucky pole". So, Dad had them switch poles. David continued to catch fish, while Jenny's empty hook, remained bare. She began to cry, and her Dad asked, "Do you know why you are not catching fish?" Jenny was convinced the shiny new hook should be enough to attract fish.

Jenny was expecting the fish to accept her concepts and thoughts. She did not consider the fish like to eat worms, but not bare metal hooks.

In organizations, churches, and classrooms today we have many leaders and teachers who are like Jenny. Many classrooms and organizational meetings are structured around the needs and desires of the teacher/leader. As Bruce Wilkinson says, "You can't force fish to bite your hook; neither can you force students to learn."

It is the fisherman who prepares and baits the hook. Fish do not bait hooks. In like manner it is the leader's (teacher's) responsibility to prepare the material to be conveyed in a manner that is interesting and relevant to our listeners.

If fish are not interested in eating green beans and potatoes, fishermen do not use them as bait. They use what will attract the fish, that bait which is interesting and relevant. As a leader, if I want my listeners to grasp, accept, and put to use the information I present, then I must prepare to deliver it in a manner that will attract their attention. If your employees, volunteers, students, are not motivated by your presentation, they'll certainly not be motivated to put it into practice.

Don't be afraid to bait your hook (prepare your presentation, even as a parent). Be sure you ae using that which is interesting and relevant to your listeners.

Leader: The Value of Learning

"The Value of learning is determined by how effectively the teacher builds comprehension, integration, and practical application." Bruce Wilkerson

As leaders we are teachers. As teachers it is our responsibility and obligation to not only impart knowledge, but also to give resources that generate relevant usage. If the information we are sharing is not transferrable in the mind of our charges (students, employees), then we are either creating trivia buffs or speaking a foreign language to them.

As memorization and comprehension of facts are important to learning and growing in our performance, being able to integrate and utilize the information should be the leader's main objective for his learners (employees). One reason people consider meetings boring is there is no practical application given with new information presented. Seldom do leaders (teachers) teach for lasting life-change. In the workforce this is a critical step oftentimes omitted from training and delivering of new information.

Dispensing information does not create lasting change, nor does it guarantee useful memorization. Memorization for memory purposes only is trivia. It may become useful, it may not. However, when we give new information along with practical uses, people catch the application and how to apply this in their performance. Adding application is not simply telling people how to use it. This would be the fastest way, but the least effective of producing retention for performance change.

Allowing time to practice is naturally the first line of application we think of. But, application can also take the form of questions ex. "How could this new technology assist you in your performance?" or "What can you see as the two greatest advantages of applying this to your situation?" Application can also be shown through stories and illustrations.

The Value of learning rests on the leader, not the learner.

There are numerous ways to assist your employees/volunteers in integrating new information, new technology, new ways into the workplace, church, or individual lives. Move away from being only a knowledge dispenser. Instead, become an organizer of learning experiences that compels people to grow with even greater effectiveness.

Vulnerability in Leadership

Many years ago, I hired in, selling vacuum cleaners, in homes. Within four weeks our office management and the owner asked me to take on the role of sales trainer. Within the next six months our office had more successful new salespeople than any other office in our nationwide company. In fact, we captured the award of number one office in our division of a worldwide corporation. While at that time I still did not consider myself to be a "leader", we had more people who came through our training classes who went on to successful sales and management careers than any other trainer in the organization. Was I an exceptionally great trainer? No, by no means. In my mind I paled in comparison to those who trained me.

As I look back on those days and many since, I believe it was not my ability as much as my vulnerability that made a difference in so many lives. Vulnerability is considered the openness to expose one's own weaknesses and susceptibility. In leadership ministry positions to this day, I try not to see myself as better or higher than anyone else. Actually, I see everyone as how they contribute in areas where I am weak. Seeing other people's strengths is a key to leadership. Helping others to see and realize their areas of strength is also key.

One of the best ways to help others understand and utilize his/her strengths is through the use of your own vulnerability. I know I am not God's gift to leadership. However, after many years, I have come to realize that God has gifted me in some areas of leadership. Even this has not been an easy factor for me to grasp. Perhaps because I know I have shortcomings and failures in my leading. Realizing these factors is a first step. Sharing your shortcomings is the beginning of vulnerability.

It becomes very beneficial for a leader to share his/her vulnerabilities to those whom he/she leads. And the way you share is the key factor which will build up or tear down the confidence and morale of others. Always share to encourage, embolden, and strengthen those you are speaking to.

When sharing your own vulnerabilities, never share to build yourself up or show how "good" you are. Always share to show you too have weaknesses and shortcomings. Share to build others up, to show they too can overcome obstacles that they may be facing. A successful leader will share his/her vulnerabilities to help others overcome obstacles and mindsets keeping them from performing at their very best.

Show me a leader who refuses to show a chink in his own armor, his weaknesses and vulnerabilities, and you will find low morale and high turnover in that leader's employees/volunteers. Showing vulnerability actually builds integrity. What will you do this week to build integrity through vulnerability.

Moving Away from Dependent Trust

Oftentimes we enter relationships, business or personal, with a trust that is based on mutual performance. That is, "I will trust you as long as you keep up your part of our working relationship. But, the minute you do not..." Trust based on mutual performance is not a lasting trust and will lead to dissension, discord, and a break up of the organization or relationship. We see this in business and in personal relationships. This false trust has led many couples to divorce, business partnerships to dissolve, and churches to split.

Trust built only on mutual performance is like trying to build a bridge out of tissue paper. It will fail. You and I will drop the ball at some point in any dependent trust relationship. It may not be major. But, there are times in our lives when we simply cannot accomplish everything in front of us. When this happens in a relationship based on dependent trust, it will always breed fear. If your trust in me is dependent on my "doing", then I will begin to fear the possibility of not upholding to your trust level. Living with this type of fear will cause a person to act in a protection mode – protecting one's self from losing the other's support. This is not healthy and will lead to collapse of the relationship, be it in business or personal.

Trust comes when we realize the other person's good toward us is not predicated on our actions or inactions. Genuine trust is not dependent on anything. It is a character trait of integrity. Trust as an integrity character trait has the other person's best interest in mind. There is no fear of a boss, pastor, or spouse with this type of trust integrity. Even when you mess up, this person is going to be there to assist you in redeeming and improving future applications.

Pastors and church leaders believe they have automatic, built-in trust. However, genuine trust comes over time. Too many religious leaders lead out of a dependent based trust without even being aware of it. Even pastors must work to build the genuine trust level with his peers and church members/volunteers.

When you build this type of trust integrity, you will see those who work for you or alongside you begin to move more freely and comfortably. Without the chains of fear, he/she will be a greater productive laborer for your organization or relationship. Don't assume that you have genuine trust integrity. Begin today, working toward building it into your character.

Building Trust Is Building Integrity

Several years ago, I read the story of a company owner who, after listening to his employees needs, promised his employees that he would get them the best insurance benefits possible. The company had budgeted a certain amount of money in expectation of health insurance costs. When the decisions were made, and the insurance plan selected, the company had saved a considerable amount of money. This is where character integrity of the owner comes in. He could have said, "We saved the money, we'll put it into the bottom line for profits," therewith lining his own pockets. But this is not what the business owner chose to do.

Instead, he decided this amount of money was budgeted for benefits and it would be used for benefits. The company placed all of the money saved from the insurance purchase, into a fund for employee retirement benefits. Of course, when this was revealed to the employees, they were ecstatic. Employee morale soared. And just as important, at least three other benefits were recognized.

The business owner's integrity was elevated among the employees. All employees understood their boss could be trusted to do what he said he would do. He had promised to get them the best insurance he could, and he did. In addition, he did it at a lower than expected cost. Trust is critical in any relationship.

Second, the employees received a bonus benefit that was totally unexpected, in their retirement. While the owner could have placed the saved money in the profit column for his own benefit, he did not. Instead, I believe he did what many businesses would not, he gave it in to his employees by placing it in their retirement funding. Taking care of your employees/volunteers is critical to high morale and improved productivity as well as retaining employees/volunteers.

Third, the employees were comforted to know they did not have to have representation in the room for every decision concerning their well-being. It is always good to get input from all levels of leadership, employees, and volunteers of your organization. However, when you build trust within the organization, people understand being outside the room does not mean their concerns are not being listened to and addressed. When trust is this strong in any organization or relationship, productivity will certainly soar.

Dr. Henry Cloud says, "If all companies (organizations, churches) were run like this, labor dispute might be an oxymoron." Wouldn't that be a dream world! Build trust in all your relationships, listen to the voice of others, keep your word, and remember, it is <u>not</u> all about the bottom line. Building trust is building Integrity!

Connecting to Retain

We've all heard of businesses with a "high-turnover" rate. Businesses that cannot seem to keep employees. Following a short term of employment, employees keep leaving the company. Normally, it is considered a fault of those leaving the company. The job was not what he expected. She just was not committed. He's not use to hard work. In some cases, this might be true.

However, when turnover continues among good, and not so good, employees, other issues need to be addressed. Great leaders will look at the inner workings of the company, the structure and atmosphere or culture inside the organization.

I have read the story of Dell computers a few years back. When internal surveys revealed that half (50%) of Dell's employees reported they would leave the company if they had an opportunity, the two top officers took notice. While many CEO's pastors, or other top officers would have dismissed or explained it away, Michael Dell and Kevin Rollins took the matter seriously. In fact they took it personally – in a good way.

Both Dell and Rollins began addressing their own weaknesses that had lowered morale in the workplace. Understanding the reality of this situation and the lengths that this CEO and President went to, gives testimony to why Dell is considered one of the best led companies in North America. One article written about the Dell experience can be found in Business Week Magazine, November 3, 2003.

Hiring or recruiting the right people is critical. But hiring the absolute best person for a position is no guarantee he/she will stay. Without connectedness (see connections post) on the leader's part, disparity will increase, and morale will decline (sometimes rapidly). With declining morale, the workplace becomes a place of anxiety and depression. No one wants to stay under those conditions.

Some of the words used (by employees) to describe Dell's two top leaders were, impersonal, detached, autocratic, antagonistic, and unapproachable. Michael Dell was an "off the charts" introvert. He had not realized the interpretation this would give to his employees. He sat out to change his own vulnerabilities right away.

Connecting with others, (getting to know his/her personal story) is the absolute best way to insure they feel understood and appreciated for their efforts. This does not require major effort or time. Simply a couple of minutes a day getting to know a little about what gets people up every morning. Every person wants to feel valued in life. To provide this connectedness to employees/volunteers requires a leader who is willing to break through his own vulnerabilities. Try connecting to understand how you can improve morale and productivity. You will also retain your valuable employees who will be your cheerleaders as well.

Building Connection Creates Trust

Jane had had enough. Her co-workers loved her. She always seemed to be able to figure out how to tackle a new issue or situation. Unfortunately, Jane's boss, the company owner, just wasn't a listener. Convinced that her ideas were not being considered after three years of employment, Jane left the company. And five other employees followed her. Morale had been low for some time. With Jane's departure, it took a nosedive.

When a person lives in any relationship long enough believing he/she is not being heard, trust disappears, separation and disappointment sets in. Each of us wants to be heard. And most of us believe we are good listeners. We operate with the belief that "I hear what my employees (volunteers, wife, friends) say." In reality unless we connect with what they are sharing, we are only surface listening. Surface listening is only listening to be polite, listening only to give our prepared respond.

In any relationship, be it work related, church, or personal, when a person has given up on being heard by the other, he/she has not given up on being heard by someone. This is where the demise of marriages, organizations, and friendships begins. If you're not listening to your spouse, she will find someone who will listen. As a corporate leader or minister, if you are not listening with an intent to connect, your people will find others who will listen, inside and out of your organization. What the others will hear, is usually not what you want them to hear.

I have been in countless meetings and read many stories where a concern was being voiced, yet the leader skimmed over the concern or gave a statistical reason why the concern was not valid. Each time we do this as leaders, our trust factor drops in the minds of those in attendance – and others who will hear from those in attendance. Building trust requires many more deposits than withdrawals.

The best way I know to build trust is to connect with those who serve alongside you and work for you. Connecting through listening does not imply building an in-depth close and personal relationship, inviting everyone to your house for dinner. It does mean listening to others with the intent to hear their concerns without a prepared answer or dismissal of his/her concern.

It is impossible to build trust without connecting with others. On the opposite side, the greater the connection, the stronger the trust factor. Think about it, whom do you trust most? Undoubtedly, one of the person's you are strongly connected with. Wise leaders understand spending a little time connecting with their charges (employees, volunteers) is worth volumes of trust.

People who trust, demonstrably will accomplish more and morale will remain high among those who trust. Invest a little time building connections. You'll create trust and be glad you did.

Lead Like a Discipler

Lucian Coleman once wrote, "*A disciple who disdains learning is no less paradoxical than a cowboy who won't go near horses.*" I find that humorous and at the same time very accurate. As we lead, our leading should always be to cause learning in those following. The word cause means to produce, initiate, or affect. Cause is defined as; *a person or thing that gives rise to an action*. Our desire should be to initiate, produce, and affect the learning of our employees/volunteers.

Jesus set a prime example for us. He selected 12 men from various backgrounds. They represented a good cross-section of the culture of the day. Mostly, unlearned men, Jesus selected men because of their potential to be leaders in His Kingdom. Various backgrounds, unlearned men with all the prejudices of the day, yet, the one attribute they each had (well at least 11) was they were teachable.

Training (equipping) those who follow us (employees/volunteers) involves 3 steps, just as Jesus demonstrated with His disciples. Successful leaders assist their followers in observing, practicing what they've learned, and then training others also. What a wonderful joy when those we have trained and equipped become the teacher for newer employees, volunteers, or church members.

In the corporate world, we have devolved to simply finding someone who needs work (or a paycheck) and placing them in a position where they have no passion, skill, or desire to work. Unfortunately, in the church we have followed the same pattern – filling an empty slot with a warm body, any warm body. This only breeds discontent and low output.

A leader is a learner and should always be pouring into those following. It will not be at the same level for each person, but willing learners are more productive. Jesus called to few men with short statements like, "Follow me." When He did these men dropped their workload and followed. Why? The reason is most of these men had already had some short interactions with Jesus. Jesus' profound leadership was clearly evidenced through these early interactions. These 12 men had already observed (the first step) Jesus' ability. He apparently demonstrated likeable leadership qualities through simple observation, to <u>cause</u> these men to want to learn and to follow Him in learning.

Is your leadership causing people to want to follow you? Those you lead are your disciples, if only for the job they are being paid. Treat them as disciples. Grow them to be the best disciples possible. They will be more productive and will also produce a positive, learning atmosphere for newcomers.

The Crave Factor

Throughout pregnancy women have cravings for particular foods. Sometimes these cravings seem peculiar to others, like pickles and ice cream, together. Truth be known, we all have cravings. Cravings for particular foods, cravings to be accepted, cravings to be the best at our jobs, cravings to have the highest skill level possible for what we enjoy.

It is these cravings that drive us forward. With the exception of the foods, these other cravings listed above propel us to improve our skills, abilities, and likeability. As leaders, we are to provide the information, resources, and tools to assist everyone in our charge in improving their personal ability assets. This will bring about effective production.

In addition, leaders should provide the source for craving. Is it possible that we are not providing the crave factor for our employees/volunteers? I believe in many instances the crave factor is missing in the workplace and in ministry. People who yearn to know a certain subject prove to be advanced learners. This yearning is a craving for knowledge and skill, a craving to be accepted and valued. This is not only in the workplace or ministry field. This craving applies to every area of life, including at home.

In the workplace and in ministry, when we, as leaders can determine the correct, needed craving and then set out to create that craving, we will see effective production from our employees/volunteers.

Too often we set the wrong craving. When we should be setting the table for steak and lobster, we are setting for bologna and cheese. Someone develops a yearning or craving for something because it is towards a goal they want, not one you thrust on them. A pregnant woman craves pickles and ice cream because the brain is reacting to the body's need for both sugar and salty-brine. Take some time and search for the correct craving.

Oftentimes we may intend to create a craving, when in fact, we are only thrusting our demands on employees/volunteers. As a leader, be the brain that sends the impulses to meet the needs of the organization. Only be certain to send impulses that create a craving (passionate desire) to meet the needs of the organization. Remembering the craving must compel each person from the inside, not the organization's point of view. When as a leader you can create this proper craving in your charges, you will see improved productivity and higher morale.

Simplify Your Directives

"I know you love fishing and you've been fishing all your lives. I realize this is how you support your family. It is your family business. But I have something else I want you to consider. You know me and have seen me around the last few weeks. I want you to leave all this behind. Stop what you are doing, leave all this behind, and join my team. Follow me around for a few years and learn. You know how to catch fish. Follow me and you'll learn how to catch men."

While the above paragraph is in parentheses, it is not an actual monologue. But if Jesus had used the business acumen of many of today's leaders, this might be how He would have recruited His Disciples. Instead, Jesus simply said, "Follow me, and I will make you fishers of men."

"Come, Follow Me." Simple, straight forward. This is a directive of Jesus Christ to His Disciples. Simple does not always mean easy. Simple is uncomplicated. Jesus' directives for His followers were usually simple, uncomplicated. Jesus used three words or less in some situations. To some of His Disciples, He said, "Follow me and I will make you fishers of men." In this scenario, His directive was accompanied with a promise. "Follow me," was the directive. The promise was "and I will make you fishers of men."

As leaders in church and the corporate world today, we often think we are giving easy to follow directives, yet our delivery or the comprehension of others complicates the directive. These complications often lead to failed attempts or a mistaken application. Either of these will end in frustration for both parties. How can we avoid these frustrations? Here are three suggestions.

1. Simplify your directives for others by using as few words as possible. Use enough words to get the objective across without being wordy.

2. Write out your directive. Writing out your directive allows you the opportunity to see and examine it word for word to ensure it is concise and direct enough to be understood.

3. Be positive in wording and delivery. As stated in earlier posts, not one of us communicates as clearly as we believe ourselves. Record your directive just as if your charges were standing in front of you. Then play it back. How did you sound? Forceful, lackadaisical, accusatory, encouraging? Now play it back for some other person who can evaluate objectively.

The easiest directive for anyone to follow is a simple, uncomplicated one. What steps will you take today to ensure your directives are simple and uncomplicated for all to follow?

All of Jesus' directives were accompanied by a promise, spoken or implied. The promise was something better than the current state. Are your directives accompanied by a promise? If so, will your promise have a positive impact on the lives of those following your directive?

Lead With Clarity

Pastor Will, speaking with one of his staff members stated, "Joseph, your team is falling behind every week. The other teams seem to be doing fine and keeping the pace. I need you and your team to step it up."

Did you notice a glaring omission in Pastor Will's statement? There is no clarity. His statement to Joseph is very vague. There is no clarity in what the goal or objective is, what Joseph's team is falling behind in, or what Joseph needs to accomplish. Whether you hold a leadership position in the church or a corporate organization, clarity is key.

I read somewhere that leadership begins with clarity. While I agree, I believe we need to clarify something (pardon the pun). Great leadership begins and ends with clarity. In fact, clarity is a character trait of great leadership.

Clarity is defined as; the quality of being clear. The quality of coherence and intelligibility. easy to see or hear; sharpness of image or sound.

Recently my wife and I were having a great start to our weekend. Then I messed it up. I wanted to show her how to check the air in her tires and how to use our compressor to add air if needed when I was not around. The mistake I made and one that many leaders make is, I was using terminology that I learned and have used since I was a child. I assumed she knew what I was talking about. She did not. This was all foreign to her.

I never raised my voice, I did not get angry or upset with my wife. However, because she did not know the language, she interpreted my reactions and verbiage as condescending and hurtful.

I have said for years that there is not one person on earth (in every walk of life) who communicates as clearly as we think we do. And I proved that fact on this particular Saturday. Having clarity as a leader is more than understanding yourself but insuring every person you are communicating with is as clear as you are on the subject.

To be clear, to have clarity as a leader, when you think you have shared your thoughts enough, share them again – and again. Share in simple terms (simple means uncomplicated, not necessarily easy). Always ask questions to ascertain if your employees/volunteers have an adequate understanding of the task ahead and how to accomplish said task. Clarity is key in communication and leadership!

Sidenote: My wife and I recovered fine from our miscommunication that morning and had a very peaceful and nice weekend together.

Tell Me More

One consideration people everywhere in our culture today have in common is, People want to be heard. Unfortunately, there are two barriers in most organizations. One is, there is no apparent structure for the average worker or member to share his/her viewpoints and suggestions. Some organizations and leaders go to extremes to make sure workers do have a communication avenue like this. Poor leaders do not want any input from others. Great, successful leaders on the other hand, welcome input and provide avenues of communication.

The second barrier is most people have difficulty expressing his/her viewpoints and suggestions. Few people have been trained or know how to deliver a suggestion without attached emotional baggage. Therefore, what could be a great suggestion, becomes a complaining point. You cannot (and should not) totally separate emotional attachment from a suggestion, especially if your belief is that this suggestion will benefit organizational quality. As leaders we need to be able to assist others in sharing his/her ideas in a congruent manner.

As a coach, I have found one of the best ways to do this is by asking a "tell me more" question. "That's interesting. Can you tell me more?" A couple others would be, "Can you unpack that for me?" "Have you seen this happen before? If so, how was it handled?" Tell me more questions allow the speaker to process a little further his/her issue and reason for speaking. This approach may take a few more minutes, but it can produce great results for the entire organization.

These questions open the door for you, the leader to ask, "How do you think we could better handle this in the future?" or "Thank you for that insight. We'll work on a better solution. If you have any thoughts, please submit them in writing, so I convey your thoughts correctly." Having someone submit possible solutions in writing causes them to think about how you as the leader have to process information. It also shows that you are interested in listening to his/her viewpoint and suggestions.

Oftentimes, the answer to this individual's personal issue will be revealed in his/her explanation. This will give the leader the information needed to help this person acheive greater effectiveness. Never underestimate the power of influence on others when they believe their voice is being heard.

Accepting the Brutal Facts of Reality

Why are we afraid of reality? It is true in business, the church, and even in our casual conversations, we obscure the reality of life. In the church we often hear, "we're doing fine." Or "We're running about the same as last year." The interpretation of the reality of these is, "We're losing ground. Not as many people coming, no new people joining, and lack of finances."

In his book *Good to Great*, Jim Collins speaks of facing the brutal facts of reality. In *Reaching the Summit*, I speak of having a *Vigorous Face to Face Summit with Reality*. In all situations of any relationship or organization, until you confront the true (often brutal) facts of reality, you will not be able to pull out of any downward spiral in the relationship or organization.

Unfortunately, many people would rather glaze over or totally ignore reality, rather than face the true and often brutal facts. We want to live in our fantasy world, believing everything will turn out alright, someday. And we believe that day is just around the corner with our next big event, the next big wave or program sweeping the nation. Brutal fact: It just does not happen!

It is seemingly human nature to hide the truth when there are potential consequences and possible risk. Many churches remain in decline because the members (and leaders) refuse to accept reality. It is often not until the church is in dire consequences they will call on someone from outside to help. In fact, the call for help is usually one of the final grasps for survival. Even then the church is looking for a savior. Reality is; the church already has a savior and does not need another savior.

If you want to find the realty of your situation, call on a trained, unbiased outsider – someone who has nothing to gain – to assist your organization in uncovering the reality of your situation and assisting in strategically planning a turnaround.

Creating a Culture of Discipline

In more than one of his books, Jim Collins writes of successful organizations having a Culture of Discipline. In *Great By Choice*, Collins remarks, "Discipline, in essence, is consistency in action. Discipline is not the same as regimentation...Discipline is not the same as hierarchical obedience or adherence to bureaucratic rules..." Giving great examples, Collins spends entire chapters in *Good to Great*, and *Great By Choice*, helping readers to understand discipline in an organization.

Discipline is not strictly following a set of rules or performing out of fear of the boss. True discipline in an organization requires independence at every level. True discipline requires an independence to avoid and steer away from those ideals and practices that would draw a person or organization into conformity with other worldviews. True organizational discipline requires individual self-discipline at every level of the organization.

Of course, this does not mean everyone has the total freedom to do his/her own thing. But if everyone is on the same page, with the same objective in mind, desiring the same outcome, then true discipline will always bring the desired result in a very effective and complementary system. Bureaucracy slows down effectiveness and production. Remove the bureaucracy and the positional leaders and you can create a culture of discipline in your organization that surpasses expectations.

With the right people in place, any organization will be filled with individuals who have the self-discipline to advance the progress of the organization. An organization with a true culture of discipline will grow more toward the discipline culture. Organizations that have adopted a culture of discipline, have even reported their "slackers" have stepped up or moved on to other organizations of their own accord.

Creating a culture of discipline is not easy, and it will take time. As with any major change in an organization, the desire to fall back into old cultures and habits is not only easy, but instinctive. It takes self-restraint and organizational restraint to remain in the culture of discipline. And the rewards are irreplaceable for years ahead.

Remember discipline is consistency in action. What freedoms can you create for your members or employees that will help you create a culture where everyone desires the same end result – a heart-felt desire for effective accomplishment of your mission?

Read more about creating a culture of discipline in Jim Collins books, *Good to Great* and *Great by Choice* or contact George Yates at SonC.A.R.E. Ministries.

Whose Mirror Are You Reflecting?

How do you see yourself? We all have a vision of how we look, who we are. You might call this our self-vision. I was recently reading something from Stephen Covey. Actually, reviewing a book I had read years ago. Covey was writing about this subject, vision or how we see our self. Covey wrote, "We all have some vision of ourselves and our future. And that vision creates consequences. More than any other factor, vision affects the choices we make and the how we spend our time."

Perhaps today more than any time in history the social mirror is clamoring for more and more reflected identity. People whose vision is based on the social mirror make choices and decisions based on what others think. Choices are made based on the expectations of others. A person whose self-vision is only a reflection of the social mirror, cannot have a personal connection to the true self, his unique abilities to develop and contribute to family and society.

The Baby-boomer generation (of which I am one), wrote its own script. Sometimes that was good, sometimes perhaps not. Even in the coming of age, Baby-boomers created its own social mirrors. Many of the social mirrors of the Baby-boomers were to reflect anything but what "the establishment" stood for. Baby-boomers have carried some of those social mirrors for 50 years.

Yet, as I look around today, I see a social mirror that is very different and extreme. And it is being cast on younger generations much by the Baby-boomer leaders in various sectors of our society.

Whether in America or any other culture, a social mirror reflection of self is always pulling people away from his/her true God-given individuality. When we are living out scripts handed to us by others we cannot honor God through our uniqueness created by Him.

With a passion to unearth your true self, the reflection in your mirror can be a prevailing motivating force to propel you beyond anything you can imagine or dream. It happened for me first, when I stopped watching the news, in 1980. I realized newscasts were negative. Of a typical thirty-minute newscast, seldom is there more than thirty seconds of anything not negative. No wonder people have such a negative perspective on life. It was not only turning off newscasts. I made a concerted effort to change my self-vision, my mirror of me.

Last week my wife and I saw a photo of a young woman whom we knew when she was a teenager. As a teenager, she saw herself as an outcast, someone who was different, unliked, undesireable. Because this is who she felt she was in society, this was her mirror, she always tried to reflect this image, and she did it well. However, the photo we saw last week revealed a beautiful young lady with a positive attitude and a drive to accomplish, even in spite of society if society tried to push back on her.

God created you a unique individual with positive qualities to accomplish that which is beyond your comprehension. Whose mirror are you reflecting, society's, or God's?

People Are Not Opposed to Change

Believe it or not ATMs (Automated Teller Machines) were introduced to us in the late 1960's. When they were first introduced most of the nation was skeptical of them. In fact, most citizens refused to use ATMs. After all, this was a far cry from the normal banking experience. Fast forward to today and many people in American society would not know how to exist without ATMs. Finding and using ATMs is now as common as walking down the street.

The introduction of ATMs was foreign to our custom of banking. Yet over time it has become part of the very fabric of banking in the United States. Acceptance of the ATM was gradual. This was change. Change is not easily accepted, is it?

Contrary to what we've been told, people are not opposed to change. However, people do not like forced change. We do not like someone else telling us we must change. Banks did not tell us we must use ATMs. ATMs were introduced alongside traditional banking practices.

Before ATMs were ever introduced, bank employees were trained to encourage customers to use ATMs. They were trained in the benefits and advantages of using ATMs. Advertisements and promotions were published promoting the safety, security, and ease of use of ATMs. Slowly ATMs were acclimated into our lives. Banks were preparing us for ATMs before the first ATM hit the market. And they continued preparing us for several years.

The way we watch TV has changed. From black & white to color. From small 9 inch to 100 inch screens. From analog to HG, to 4K resolution. From using dials on the TV to remotes to smart TVs. All of these are changes that have happened in our lifetime. Change is inevitable, and people have adapted and accepted these changes without recourse.

People have adapted to change their entire lives. It is not change that people fear or are opposed to. It is forced change. As leaders, we are to guide and to, well, lead people into change. Too often organizational change is forced change. When leaders take the time to educate and bring people along, change can move much smoother than it often does.

We need to take a lesson from the banking industry. We need to slowly educate – long before the coming change. Educate, equip, and train our workers, employees, customers, members in a slow methodical process. Take your time; investigate, explore, train, equip, and implement in due time. Don't rush change. Guide people bringing them along with openness and honesty.

Change will come and the ease of change will be like money from an ATM.

Stretching Beyond your Comfort Zone

As a boy growing up in a small cape cod style house, my three brothers and I slept upstairs in our home. Our upstairs consisted of two open-air rooms. My oldest brother slept in the smaller room at the left of the staircase. My next older brother and I shared the larger of the two rooms at the right side of the stairs. My youngest brother slept at the top of the stairs on a small bed. I remember at least one night after the lights were out, my two older brothers (I of course would not be involved) would slip out of their beds and crawl across the floor quietly sneaking up to my younger brother's bed and pop up suddenly and scare him.

To hide from his fears my younger brother would pull the covers up over his head until he would stop shaking and felt it was safe to pull the covers down. Of course, it would only be a few minutes until one of the older ones was there at his bed again.

I remember thinking, "How is that going to save you?" But in my brother's mind, his bed was his safe haven. Pulling his cover over his head provided his safety zone – his comfort zone. As long as he was in his bed with his cover he felt safe and comfortable.

Pulling your covers over your head may keep you from facing your fears. It will not help you out of your comfort zone. <u>It will never take you where God wants to lead you</u>!

Most professed Christians never truly experience being on-mission with God because they will not pull the covers down from over their head. No growth ever takes place in your comfort zone. God stretches you. He wants you to get out of your comfort zone so He can bless you with all the blessings of heaven (Ephesians 1:3-4).

We have got to not only pull the covers down to see where God is at work, we need to get out of that nice, warm, comfortable bed and join God in His work.

After all, what is the purpose of the church? The purpose of the church (God's people) always has been and always will be to be "On Mission" with God to the unchurched.

Our marching orders are stated in Matthew 28:19-20. "GO" it says. That word means as you are going, As you go through life, you are to do the following... *Who* are we to go with? JESUS. He said at the end of those verses that He will always be with us even to the end of the earth.

To be On-Mission with God means that we are to be about God's business. Not the business we think would please God. To do this we must be willing to get out of our comfort zone – out of that nice warm comfortable bed (or pew) and join God in the work He is doing around us. Therein comes the joy and the blessings of heaven.

Stalwart & Steadfast

In all areas of life and ministry, we confront adversarial situations. As I read about and study the great heroes of faith, successful organizations, and entrepreneurs, I see a common thread. This common bond or thread as I see it is a twofold character trait. While each of these two facets are great qualities and can stand alone, together they solidify a man's temperament and resolve. These two character traits are a stalwart belief and a steadfast faith.

Standing stalwart in your beliefs and steadfast in yourfaith will carry a man farther than skill, ability, or fortune. Those finding themselves in an adversarial position may not be able to rely on fortune, skill, or ability. The two elements that can be relied upon are belief in a successful outcome and a faith to carry on through the difficulty. One thought that may come to mind here is that the outcome might not be the "successful" outcome we perceive or desire. However, God's ways are much greater than our ways and His thoughts higher than ours. Therefore, it is worthy to always look at the outcome and see it from God's kingdom perspective.

One of the great men of faith from the first century is the apostle Paul. Reading some of the words of the apostle Paul from the New Testament gives us insight into a man who was both stalwart in belief and steadfast in his faith.

Five times I received from the Jews 40 lashes minus one.
Three times I was beaten with rods. Once I was stoned.
Three times I was shipwrecked. I have spent a night
and a day in the depths of the sea. On frequent journeys,
[I faced] dangers from rivers, dangers
from robbers, dangers from my own people, dangers
from the Gentiles, dangers in the city, dangers
in the open country, dangers on the sea,

and dangers among false brothers; labor and hardship, many sleepless nights, hunger and thirst, often without food, cold, and lacking clothing. Not to mention other things, there is the daily pressure on me: my care for all the churches (2 Corinthians 11:24–28).

The apostle Paul suffered all these things, yet he always had words to share of his love and devotion to the God he served. Paul was stalwart in his journey, always pressing on, no matter what hardships he faced. He never stopped, suffering through all these things. Even after all this torture, pain, and hardship, Paul was found singing and praising God in prison, witnessing to the guards and writing letters of encouragement and training to the churches he had helped to start. He didn't complain. Instead, in his own words Paul said, "*I press on*" (Philippians 3:14 NIV). Paul was stalwart in his belief and steadfast in his faith, never wavering.

God has promised He will never leave nor forsake you. He is with you every day, all day. Jesus, in the last words of the Great Commission, said, "*I am with you always, even unto the end of the world*" (KJV). You have what it takes to build a stalwart belief and steadfast faith. Stand on the shoulders of those who have gone before so that you will be strengthened for the victory and your shoulders will be broadened for those who come after you.

Remember, there are three more volumes of 510 Elevate Life & Leadership. Which will you begin reading tomorrow?

Made in the USA
Columbia, SC
01 May 2023